The Summer Camp

HANDBOOK

Everything you need to find, choose, and get ready for overnight camp —and skip the homesickness

Christopher A. Thurber, PhD
Jon C. Malinowski, PhD
Illustrated by Mark Scott

Perspective Publishing
Los Angeles

5942719

Library of Congress Catalogue Card Number: 99-087850
ISBN: 1-930085-00-1

Published by Perspective Publishing, Inc.
2528 Sleepy Hollow Dr. #A, Glendale, CA 91206
800-330-5851; 818-502-1270; fax: 818-502-1272;
books@familyhelp.com or perspectivepub@loop.com
www.familyhelp.com

Additional copies of this book may be ordered by calling toll free
1-800-330-5851, or by sending $18.95 ($14.95 + $4 shipping) to the above
address. CA residents add 8.25% ($1.23) sales tax. Discounts available for
quantity orders. Bookstores, please call LPC Group at 1-800-626-4330.

Library of Congress Cataloging-in-Publication Data

Thurber, Christopher A., 1968-
    The summer camp handbook : everything you need to find, choose, and
    get ready for overnight camp—and skip the homesickness / Christopher
    A. Thurber, Jon C. Malinowski; illustrated by Mark Scott.—1st ed.
       p.cm
    Includes bibliographical reference and index.
    ISBN 1-930085-00-1
       1. Camps—United States—Handbooks, manuals, etc. I. Malinowski,
    Jon C., 1969- II. Title
    GV193.T58 2000
    796.54'22—dc21   99-087850

Illustrations by Mark Scott
Back cover photo by Christiaan P. Vorkink
Printed in the United States
First Edition

To our friends under the pines

Acknowledgements

Writing a book is a demanding task rendered exhilarating by the assistance and encouragement of others. We thank our parents, for their wisdom in sending us to camp; Simonida, for her love and for understanding our obsession; Gene and Caryn, guardians of Camelot, for their loyalty and guidance; Tom, for perennially nurturing our leadership abilities; Louise, Chuck, Jan, Chas, Byron, Rob, Mark, Bob, Judy, Susan, Ruth, and other reviewers for their excellent comments; the cabin leaders who helped us collect data, gave us suggestions, and made us laugh over the years; our graduate and postdoctoral advisors, Drs. Marian Sigman, John Weisz, David Patterson, Wil Gesler, and John Florin, for letting us take a road less traveled; Linda, for her editorial skills; and all the campers who helped us seek the joy of being alive.

Table of Contents

PART I

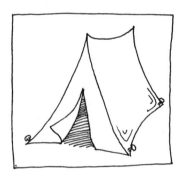

THE CAMP
EXPERIENCE

CHAPTER 1

How this book will help

In the forest behind the cabins, the 260 campers around the fire fell suddenly silent. Some shifted on the wooden benches where generations of campers had gathered before them. Others looked intently at the flames, whose orange light danced on their young faces. The session was over, and only the candlelight ceremony remained before the campers would pack their sleeping bags and their memories and head home. Some would remember the cabin leader who sailed the lake with them on a perfect summer afternoon. Others would remember the first bull's-eye they hit on the archery range. A few would recall sitting with their friends watching the sunset deepen from pink to crimson. One by one, the campers blew out their candles, but no one would ever extinguish the magic of overnight camp.

For more than 140 years, parents have given their children the gift of an overnight camp stay. As with any meaningful gift, this one takes some thought. *The Summer Camp Handbook* is what you need to find the best camp and help your child get the most out of it. You'll learn

- What makes overnight camp special
- How to know when the time is right for overnight camp

- The key differences between traditional, specialty, and special needs camps
- How to decide on the best location and length of stay
- What kind of activity structure best suits your child
- Where to find the most up-to-date information on overnight camps
- How to evaluate promotional materials that camps send you
- Important questions to ask the camp director
- How to find a camp that matches your child's interests and skills
- How parents and children can manage homesickness
- What issues you should discuss with the camp nurse or doctor
- Tips for packing, no matter what kind of camp you choose
- How to have smooth opening and closing days of camp
- What a care package is and what makes a good one
- The best ways parents and children can keep in touch
- Strategies kids can use to maximize their fun at camp

What this book is

The Summer Camp Handbook is different from any other camp resource book or World Wide Web page in four important ways:

1. The authors are camping professionals who still work at overnight camps. Together, we have more than 45 years of camping experience. We've both been campers, cabin leaders, instructors, and senior staff members. We know what works and what doesn't work. We know what kids like and don't like.

2. This book is based on years of researching the overnight camp experience. Because we are also academics, we like to back up what we say with hard data. The wisdom in this book is based on our findings about what children and parents can do to enhance their camp experience.

3. We'll give you insider tips on how to select, prepare for, and enjoy overnight camp, but we won't list every camp in the country. That list changes every year. Instead, we'll share our unique step-by-step method of selecting the best camp for you. We'll show you how to evaluate the most up-to-date information available from camps, the Internet, the library, and even your friends.

4. *The Summer Camp Handbook* is a book for families. Anyone in the family is welcome to read any of the chapters. However, we wrote Parts I–IV especially for parents, because they're the ones who do most of the searching and paying for camps. In Part V, you'll find a chapter written just for kids, plus a lot of helpful extras for families. Throughout the book, you'll find many helpful checklists for parents and a sprinkling of fun text boxes for kids.

Getting the most out of this book

To get the most out of this book, we recommend that you read it cover-to-cover 6 to 12 months before the camp season. That may seem like a long time ahead, but if you're starting from square one, you'll be researching camps, making a selection, scheduling a physical exam, getting emotionally prepared for the separation, learning how to pack, and finishing dozens of miscellaneous tasks. It's a lot to do, especially when you consider that most camps fill up their available bunks several months before they open. Therefore, it's a good idea to start the selection process now and register early for the camp you eventually choose.

For those of you pressed for time, this is just the book for you. Although it is a comprehensive and thorough reference, we've also written the book with your busy lifestyle in mind. You can go to the table of contents and index, pinpoint the information you need now, and just read that. In addition, most chapters have summaries of key information.

If you are reading this and camp opens in less than six months, fear not. We have arranged the chapters chronologically, so you can jump in at any stage of the game. You can either read the entire book to see whether you've forgotten anything, or you can go directly to the chapters that interest you. There is still time to make wise choices. Your future camper should read the *Just for kids* section as soon as possible.

If you've already chosen a camp, congratulations! It's not an easy choice, considering all the possibilities. We recommend skimming

Parts I and II of the book to see what else you might learn about the camp you chose. Then, parents should read Parts III and IV more closely, and kids should read the *Just for kids* section. These contain important discussions about the emotional and physical preparation that helps so much before camp starts. You'll also find tips on packing and preparing for a smooth opening day.

If your child is already at camp, skim Part III and carefully read Part IV. There, you'll find a lot of information on helping your child get

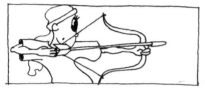

the most out of camp. We've even included sample letters to help you write supportive correspondence. You'll also find suggestions for what to include in a care package and how to prepare for a smooth closing day. You might also read *Just for kids* at the end, where you'll find helpful tips to share with your child in your next letter.

Meet the authors

Christopher Thurber

I grew up in Maine and started day camp there at age six. I remember on rainy days we'd play with toys inside, and on sunny days we'd go to the beach. I loved it. A couple of years later, I switched to a different day camp that employed an incompetent crew who failed to intervene when the big kids harassed me. Suddenly, I hated camp and stopped going.

After a few years in the Cub Scouts, my curiosity about overnight camp grew. *There must be some good camps out there*, I thought, *but two weeks is a long time to be away from home.* Only after considerable encouragement from one of my best friends did I finally try overnight camp at the age of 12. I fell in love with camp again. My cabin leader was fantastic, and I met some really nice kids, including my co-author, Jon. When my parents came to pick me up, the first words out of my mouth were, "Next summer, I want to come for four weeks!"

At 15, I served as a junior leader, and at 16, a leader-in-training. After my first summer as a full-fledged cabin leader, I wrote all my college application essays about how much camp meant to me. I knew then that I wanted to spend the rest of my life working with kids. I spent several years as a cabin leader and then served as Division Head and Waterfront Director. With my increased responsibility came more complex leadership issues and more difficult camper problems. Ultimately, these challenges led me to change my major at Harvard from government to psychology, and then to pursue my Ph.D. in clinical child psychology at the University of California, Los Angeles.

As an academic psychologist, I've spent most of my career researching the causes of, consequences of, and best ways to deal with homesickness. I've published a dozen articles on the topic and have collaborated with Jon on several studies of children's favorite places at camp. I've also had the privilege of sharing my research with hundreds of psychologists and camping professionals across the country. Like every clinical psychologist, I strive to engender positive changes in people's lives. Camp's influence on my personal and professional development is immeasurable, so it feels good to give something back.

Jon Malinowski

I grew up in Vermont and started day camp there when I was seven. I don't remember much about the experience except riding the bus to camp, feeling nervous about changing in the pool locker room, and singing the Titanic song ("It was sad when the gray ship went down. Kerplunk. It sunk. Now it's nothin' but junk!"). I must have enjoyed day camp though, because I graduated to overnight camp at age nine. I remember a few things from those first two summers at overnight camp: taking the swim check, getting sick, and witnessing older cabins raid younger cabins. My parents eventually realized that they could find someplace better.

The next year, we chose a camp where some of my friends went, and where my Cub Scout den mother sent her own children. I still remember driving up to my cabin and meeting my first leader, Jim. That summer was filled with wonderful memories and the pleasant realization that all camps are not the same. After four years as a camper there, I was asked to join the leadership. I felt privileged to be part of such a qualified group of people. After a two-year training program, I became a full-fledged cabin leader and later a senior staff member. Twenty years after my first summer there, I'm still on the staff. I've held positions as a Senior Staff member, Division Head, and Program Director. This variety has given me a valuable range of experience with campers, cabin leaders, and administrative staff. I see and experience camp from many different angles.

During four years as an undergraduate at Georgetown University and four years in graduate school at the University of North Carolina, Chapel Hill, I spent my summers at camp. In graduate school, I was working on a Ph.D. in behavioral geography, so it seemed natural to focus my doctoral dissertation on children's place preferences at overnight camp. My research made me realize that, even during a short stay at camp, children can develop strong ties with camp places, and that they use those places to deal with both the good times and the bad. I now have the honor of teaching geography at the United States Military Academy, which, ironically, is a lot like an overnight camp, although with a slightly different purpose. My years at camp have been a life-changing journey. Next to my parents, overnight camp is the single most positive thing in my life. As my co-author Chris once said, "I've got the best job in the world: I live on a baseball field."

. . .

As you can see, we have similar backgrounds in camping and academics. It's no wonder that our friendship has lasted so long. It is sort of funny, though, that it took us so long to think of writing this book. We've been telling each other for years that parents and kids would enjoy camping more if they knew more. Now that research has helped us find solutions to some of the most common questions and problems that parents and kids have concerning selecting, packing, and getting ready for overnight camp, families can be much better prepared. By reading *The*

Summer Camp Handbook, you can greatly increase the chances that you and your child will choose a camp wisely and enjoy the whole experience.

We often think back to a particularly humbling moment during the summer of 1985. We were both proud first-year cabin leaders. On the way back to our cabins one afternoon, we came across a teary-eyed boy sitting at the foot of a tall white pine. "Can you help me?" he sobbed, "I'm really homesick." We assured him that we could help, and took turns offering him comforting advice, but deep down we weren't as confident as we sounded. Suddenly, we didn't feel so proud. What could we do, really?

Fortunately, we now know what makes young people homesick and what makes them feel better when it hurts. We also know much more about how kids interact with the environment at camp and what places and activities make them happy. We don't have all the answers, but everything we do know about helping children enjoy camp is in this book, for you.

Some Notes on the Terminology and Writing Style in this Book

Overnight. In the camping industry, sleep-away or overnight camps are called resident camps, because children reside there, instead of going home each night as they do at day camp. Although some camps do use the term resident, this word has other meanings too. Therefore, we use the more specific term, *overnight*. Although most overnight camps are in session during the summer, some happen during the winter. To be inclusive, we say *overnight camp*, not *summer camp*.

Staff & Senior Staff. There are a lot of people who work at camp. Collectively, they are called staff. Directors, assistant directors, program directors, waterfront directors, and other people who are in charge at camp are called senior staff.

Cabins & Cabin Mates. Camps have different names for the different forms of housing in which children live at camp. They can be called cabins, tents, teepees, bunks, dorms, huts, lodges, or even yurts. We use the traditional word *cabin* to refer to any and all group living facilities at overnight camp. The children who live together in a cabin are called cabin mates.

Cabin Leader. The person who lives and has meals with a camper and his cabin mates is the cabin leader. Although *counselor* is also a common term, we prefer the specific term *cabin leader* because *counselor* can also mean *psychologist* or *guidance counselor* or even *lawyer*. Plus, a good cabin leader spends much more time leading than counseling.

Instructors. Some camps have staff that work only in certain activity areas, but do not live and eat with the campers. Examples of these staff members include the tennis pro, the riding instructor, and the swimming coach. We refer to these specialized staff members as instructors. Many specially trained cabin leaders are also instructors.

Pronouns. We interchange *his* and *her* and *he* and *she* throughout the book to be fair and to avoid awkward sentences. Unless specifically mentioned, all of the material in this book applies equally to boys and girls.

CHAPTER 2

Why go to overnight camp?

Sometimes I sit down by myself, like on the rocks by the brook . . . and just think about home . . . and just think how lucky I am to have parents who send me to camp. — Geordie, age 11

First of all, camp is not school. As if that's not reason enough for kids to love it, overnight camps also offer outdoor activities that most kids don't have at home or school. Plus, there are opportunities to make new friends in a relaxed environment, and positive adult role models whose priority is to show kids a good time. A good camp is kid heaven. Overnight camp also offers the unique experience of community living away from home. That experience is what makes overnight camp so special. It's what makes camp a wonderful, life-changing experience.

Spending a significant amount of time away from home is not a decision to be taken lightly or to be made unilaterally. You should include your child in the decision to go to overnight camp. Our research has repeatedly shown that children who feel included in the decision to spend time away from home adjust better than those who feel the decision was made for them.

As you read through this chapter, discuss your family's goals for camp. You may be surprised to learn that your child's goals differ from your own. That's OK. What's important is that you recognize that kids are more likely to have immediate and tangible goals, such as having fun or getting better at soccer, whereas parents are more likely to have lofty goals, such as developing social skills or nurturing independence.

Having lofty goals is commendable. After all, you're paying good money for your child to have this experience, right? Just don't forget: Having fun is Goal 1. It is the prerequisite for all the other goals you might have. Unless kids enjoy their time at overnight camp, they are unlikely to experience the personal growth you're hoping for. It's the pleasure of living at camp that paves the way for lifelong learning, such as overcoming adversity, sharing personal experiences, rising to meet challenges, and gaining self-confidence.

What kids say about why they go

Kids produce revealing answers to the question, "Why go to overnight camp?" Their opinions are as diverse as the camps they attend. Here's a small sampling, culled from the hundreds of interviews we've done as part of our research.

Camp is just awesome. I mean, there are so many things to do here that I can't do at home, like archery and horseback riding. What would I be doing if I was at home? Watching TV? —Alex, age 8

Most of my best friends are from camp. When you live with eight other girls in a cabin for four weeks, you just get close, like really bonded. That's why I come back each year. We do everything together when we're here. We even write to each other during the winter. —Emilie, age 14

At my school, it's not really challenging...not in the same way it is here at camp. At school, we have homework and stuff, but not ropes courses or learning about nature. The counselors here teach you way more than regular teachers at school. —Byron, age 13

I like being away from home. I mean, I still feel homesick sometimes and miss my parents...well, mostly Cactus. That's my dog. But it's cool to be out in the woods, kind of living on my own. —Richard, age 10

I like camp because you're not in the city, where all the buildings and smoke and noise are. And the trees here...you're in the trees, and it makes it look pretty.   —Hali, age 9

There is so much pressure at school, like homework and what you wear and who your friends are. I hate seventh grade. At camp, I'm much more myself.
—Amy, age 12

I didn't know what a church camp would be like. I thought it might be weird, but it's neat. At school, I always have to explain my religion to people, but here, all the kids are the same. I mean, the kids are all different, but we all believe in God in the same way, and that makes it easy to get along and talk.
—Elias, age 13

I've gotten so much better at soccer since I got here. The coaches are really nice and they help me a lot with my dribbling. When I first got here, I couldn't dribble at all, and this week our team won the tournament.
—Charlie, age 8

The best part, besides all the awesome stuff to do, is the cabin leaders. I can tell my leader anything and she always has time to listen. If I'm feeling sad, she usually says something to make me feel better. The leaders here are like your parents away from home. Someday, I'll be a leader here.
—Sophie, age 11

The goals of overnight camping

Let's get specific. Overnight camping has six primary goals:

1. Have fun
2. Improve athletic, artistic, and intellectual skills
3. Nurture independence
4. Make friends and develop social skills
5. Experience a new environment
6. Learn from a positive adult role model

Although some of these goals could be met at day camp, they are easiest to accomplish at overnight camp, especially Goals 3, 4, 5 and 6. The unique experience of community living away from home is a powerful force for nurturing independence, making lifelong friends, and developing social skills. Living in a new environment, especially a beautiful natural one, intensifies this experience because it's so different from home and school. Since their inception, overnight camps have been designed to build character. The good ones still do. Here's how:

Goal 1: Have fun

Camps are fun factories. Skilled camp directors and cabin leaders know how to create fun activities, regardless of the facilities they have. A good cabin leader can get a group of children excited about cleaning the cabin or picking up firewood. That may sound silly, but consider the positive example that a cabin leader sets for your child by turning an otherwise mundane activity into a fun game. You may laugh and say, "Not my kid," but we've had parents tell us how flabbergasted they were to find their children cleaning up at home, without being asked, after returning from overnight camp.

Although skilled staff and choice facilities make it easy to have fun, it's still important to check out any camp's list of activities. The range and quality of activities vary from one camp to another, but few homes or schools can offer the variety of equipment, activities, and playmates that most overnight camps do. That's why Goal 1 will be easy for your child to achieve.

Goal 2: Improve athletic, artistic and intellectual skills

Whether the camp you and your child choose offers five or five hundred activities, there will always be the opportunity to improve various skills. Of course, camps vary in the expertise of their cabin leaders and instructors. At some music camps, the instructors all have degrees from music schools, while at other music camps, the instructors are self-taught amateurs. At some traditional camps, the soccer coach is a former Division 1 All-American; at others, he is simply the guy who raised his hand a week ago and volunteered to run the program.

Who can best help your child develop skills? It's hard to say. The music school graduate and the all-star athlete obviously have the skills, but are they good teachers? Will they set a good example for your child to follow, or are they prone to losing their temper and using profanity around campers? Do they emphasize competitive achievement or personal improvement? Clearly, when it comes to helping your child achieve Goal 2, the personal qualifications of a cabin leader or instructor are as important as her athletic, artistic, and intellectual qualifications.

Besides having staff with a winning combination of personality and expertise, the camp must have sessions long enough to allow children to develop their skills. One week or more is usually enough time to achieve Goal 2. Of course, the longer the session, the more opportunities children have to develop skills. Ultimately, this skill development leads to an enhanced sense of self-worth.

At overnight camp, kids have wonderful opportunities both to master skills they already possess and to challenge themselves to develop skills in an area previously unfamiliar to them. Encourage your child to try some activities completely new to him, such as archery, sailing, acting, or ceramics. All kids—those with expertise, those with few skills, and those with special needs—will find the rewards of learning plentiful at overnight camp.

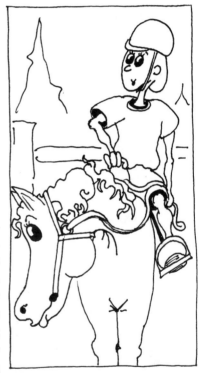

Goal 3: Nurture independence

New skills are easy to see, but newfound independence shows itself in subtle ways. When kids meet Goal 3, they become more interested in exploring things on their own and, in certain ways, less dependent on their parents. However, healthy independence does not involve severing family ties. It involves gaining the courage to explore new relationships, take healthy risks, and learn about who you are. When kids mature in these ways, they become more confident in setting and achieving important goals, taking initiative with responsibilities, and solving problems.

Goal 3 often bears fruit as soon as children return home. Parents we know love to tell the story about how, when their child returned from his first two weeks at overnight camp, he had learned to keep his elbows off the dinner table. He even started making his bed every morning!

Discoveries like this amaze parents, especially those who have given up trying to get their child to perform chores spontaneously. Of course, such increased responsibility and politeness may not last all year. Kids are kids, and camp won't change that (thank goodness!). However, camp does help kids take steps in the right direction. The responsibility they're given at camp cultivates an awareness of what needs to be done, without being told. Independence slowly evolves.

Another bonus of overnight camp is that it gives parents and kids a break from one another. Every family can use a change of pace now and then.

Goal 4: Make friends and develop social skills

Camp brochures are full of mission statements that emphasize the development of friendships and social skills. Most also emphasize the cultivation of spirituality and independence. Although these mission statements may sound grand or trite, they are true of many overnight camps. Living away from home with other kids in a rural setting does indeed promote a unique sort of personal growth. Kids learn to get along better with others, and they gain confidence in their ability to negotiate new social challenges on their own. These are critical skills. No individual can accomplish much without knowing how to get along with others.

Years after he was a camper, a friend captured the essence of Goal 4:

One of the best parts about my camp experience was the opportunity to establish myself among peers with a clean slate. None of the kids who knew me from school were there, and the authority figures had no history with me.

I felt very free to be myself, and not to be part of an ingrained social order.

When kids live with a group of their peers under the supervision of positive adult role models, their care and concern for others increases. This sense of kinship solidifies lessons about sportsmanship, sharing, and responsibility. Most important, the experience forges bonds of friendship that last a lifetime.

What About Self-Esteem and Self-Confidence?

Developing athletic, artistic, intellectual, and social skills is an especially worthy goal because these skills give children a feeling of competence. This feeling of "I can do it!" enhances their self-image and makes them truly happy. Athletic, artistic, intellectual, and social activities also allow children to express feelings, be creative, test their limits, and vent energy, which feels good.

At a properly designed and well-run camp, your child is likely to experience increases in self-esteem and self-confidence. However, you should understand that self-esteem and self-confidence are not things that anyone can simply give to a child, or that a child can consciously strive to achieve. (That's why we haven't included these concepts among the goals of overnight camp.) Instead, self-esteem and self-confidence are things children spontaneously experience after attaining some of the main goals of overnight camp. When young people have fun, build skills, nurture independence, make friends, experience a new environment, and learn from positive adult role models, self-esteem and self-confidence naturally follow.

Recent research by Randall Grayson and Paul Marsh supports the conventional wisdom that overnight camp boosts children's self-esteem. The effects are particularly strong for young children, first- and second-year campers, and for those starting with lower levels of self-esteem before camp. Those camps whose programs and philosophy intentionally focus on self-enhancement were found to make the most positive contribution to children's self-esteem.

Long after camp ends, children continue to benefit from their increased self-esteem. They often have an easier time during the school year. They may find it easier to make friends, try out for a play, or join a school club. Or, they simply may find that they are not the last one picked for the kickball team during recess. That feels good, too.

Goal 5: Experience a new environment

Since the late 1800s, parents have wanted their children to attend overnight camp simply because it is a new environment, sheltered from the vices of popular culture. A good camp has no unsavory pop icons, illegal drugs, superficial commercialism, foul language, or sexist stereotypes. Instead, you'll find a caring staff, healthy food and activities,

Outdoor Experiences Can Be Restorative

The work of Rachel and Stephen Kaplan indicates that outdoor experiences can be restorative to one's mind, body, and spirit. The Kaplans define a *restorative environment* as one containing these four components:

1. Being away—it's an escape from the everyday environment
2. Fascination—it's an experience of something interesting
3. Coherence—it's a setting that is of considerable scope to function as another world
4. Compatibility—it's a place that fits well with an individual's needs and inclinations

Certainly, many camps fit the Kaplans' definition of a restorative environment. All of the goals of overnight camping are easier to achieve in a beautiful, natural setting. For some children, outdoor living is even spiritually moving.

an appreciation for nature, and a supportive atmosphere that helps boys and girls to be both strong and caring.

Despite many changes in the camping world in the last 140 years, most camps still embrace the natural environment as a vital aspect of their programs. In fact, one of the reasons that overnight camps became so popular was that parents in the city wanted their children to get a taste of wholesome country living. If you look through *Camping Magazine* or a selection of camp brochures, you're sure to see photographs of smiling kids in front of pristine lakes, tall trees, or majestic mountains. One reason these settings have remained popular spots for overnight camps is because of kids' dwindling contact with beautiful natural environments.

At a good overnight camp, your child can gain respect for and curiosity about nature. Roughly half of all overnight camps report that they include some sort of environmental education in their daily program. The belief in nature as vital to overnight camping is evident in the American Camping Association's definition of camping: ". . . a creative recreational and educational opportunity in group living in the outdoors. [Camping] utilizes . . . the resources of the natural surroundings to contribute to each camper's mental, physical, social, and spiritual growth."

Each child finds something special in the camp environment. In one of our studies, we found that 8 to 10-year-olds prefer places in camp because of their physical properties or because of the activity that happens at that place. A 9-year-old might say that her favorite place in camp is the waterfront because she loves swimming. However, older children prefer places because of their aesthetic qualities. A 14-year-old might say that her favorite place in camp is the rowboat dock because it's the best place to see the spectacular sunsets. Given the choice, young people prefer camps with pleasant, varied landscapes.

Some camps, such as those on college campuses, have few natural landscapes. Although this is not ideal, keep in mind that your child's experience with a new, mostly artificial environment can still be beneficial. Research on something called *wayfinding* suggests that when children learn their way around one new environment, they are better at finding their way around the next new environment.

Goal 6: Learn from positive adult role models

There is one more goal of overnight camping. It's not a goal that most kids think about, but it should be on the mind of every dedicated staff member at camp: Learning from a positive adult role model. Dedicated staff members want to be positive role models, and they want children to learn from them. It is the quality of the camp staff, coupled with your child's motivation, that will determine whether she achieves any of the goals of overnight camp. Without positive adult role models, none of the other goals can be fulfilled.

At this point, you might say, "Kids learn from their parents. Why do they need other role models?" There are two answers to this question. First, kids can and do learn from their parents, but even the best parent has limitations. Other positive adult role models can support, counsel, and lead your child in surprising ways that complement your own style.

Second, the mere fact that cabin leaders are *not* their parents changes kids' outlooks. They behave differently when their parents aren't around. They explore and take risks in different ways. They reach out for friendship and security, and find it, in ways they never attempted before. Although they are authority figures, cabin leaders also function as campers' peers. They are closer to campers' ages than parents, and they can be especially playful and goofy. Considering the tremendous influence that peer groups have on children's development, parents should work hard to find a camp where the cabin leaders serve as positive role models.

At the camp where we work, the guiding principle of our staff is leadership by example, or L.B.E. Each staff member is constantly striving to set a good example, knowing that kids emulate adults' behavior, be it good or bad. Cabin leaders use proper manners, clean language, and good sportsmanship. They never ask a camper to do something that they themselves would not be willing to do. Perhaps the best example of L.B.E. that we ever saw was a bleary-eyed cabin leader who began picking up trash one morning after some raccoons had ransacked the camp dumpsters. He didn't whisper a single obscenity, nor did he solicit anyone's help. Yet within five minutes, there were 10 or 12 kids helping him throw all that disgusting trash back in the dumpster. His L.B.E. was his demonstrated willingness to do the right thing, even if it meant getting dirty. Campers respect leaders like that.

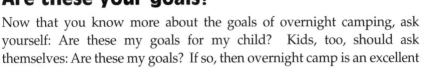

Are these your goals?

Now that you know more about the goals of overnight camping, ask yourself: Are these my goals for my child? Kids, too, should ask themselves: Are these my goals? If so, then overnight camp is an excellent choice.

However, overnight camp is not for everyone. If the goals we've outlined above are incompatible with your own, or if they don't seem to match your style, then you may wish to consider other options for leisure time. These include day camp, extended stays with friends or relatives, a family vacation, various academic programs, community theater and art programs, lessons in a favorite activity, Boy Scout, Girl Scout, or Camp Fire day programs, religious group activities, or some type of team or club, such as 4-H. Of course, you could also choose to do some of these alternatives *and* overnight camp.

CHAPTER 3

Knowing when the time is right

Kids themselves are the best judges of when they are

ready. When they show spontaneous interest in camp, that's a good clue that the time is right. Sometimes, kids' interest is sparked by a friend who has been to overnight camp. Other times, kids become excited about overnight camp after seeing an attractive camp in a brochure or on television. Other kids have parents or grandparents who generate interest by describing their own childhood experiences. Some families may suggest camp as an option after noticing that their child is bored or restless during school vacations.

Kids listen to other kids when it comes to figuring out what's fun. If you're interested in sending your child to overnight camp, but you yourself never went to camp, find a veteran camper who is your child's age. Perhaps the son or daughter of one of your co-workers or neighbors went to camp last year and enjoyed it. Arrange a time when your kids can get together and bring up the topic of overnight camp. That veteran camper will probably be better than you or any other grown-up who's never been to camp at describing the experience.

What if your child doesn't seem interested in camp, but you think it would be a good idea? First, find out the reason why she's not interested.

You might say, "You know, a lot of kids, like your friend Sarah, really love overnight camp. What do you think about going for a couple of weeks?" Your child's answer will help you figure out why she is hesitating. Is she worried about separating from home, doubting whether she'll enjoy the activities, or feeling anxious about making new friends? Whatever the reason, you should address her concern, instead of simply encouraging her to go, or worse yet, forcing her to go. Having your child talk to a peer who went to camp and loved it is powerfully persuasive. Visiting a camp while it's in session is an even more effective way to help your child lower her anxiety and boost her enthusiasm. Remember, it has to be partly her decision, not just yours.

What age is best?

We recommend that children be at least seven years old before spending a week or more at overnight camp. In general, younger children have more of a struggle than older children adjusting to the separation from home. However, there are many differences in individual children's preferences, enthusiasm, maturity, and ability to tolerate separations. Therefore, your child might be slightly younger than seven or substantially older than seven before he feels comfortable going to overnight camp. There is no right age at which all children are ready for overnight camp.

Besides your child's age, you should also consider both the age range and age distribution of the other campers. A camp may say that it enrolls children between 8 and 16, but if there are only two eight-year-olds out of several hundred campers, the camp is probably geared toward older kids. Find a camp where there are lots of children the same age as your child.

As you read through the following sections, keep in mind that you have the option to choose different camps throughout your son's or daughter's childhood and adolescence. Some kids start with an overnight camp that has short stays and is close to home, and then transition to a camp that has longer stays and is farther away. Other kids start with camp that has a broad, general program of activities, and then try a camp with a specialized program. Of course, there are also kids who begin at one camp and fall in love with it. Kids at these camps may start at age 7 or 8 and return every year until they are 15 or 16. It isn't unusual for such campers to become cabin leaders or instructors at that same camp.

What about length of stay?

Session length is partly determined by the age of the youngest campers. Traditional camps with two-week sessions usually don't accept boys and girls younger than seven or eight, whereas camps that offer two or three-day sessions will sometimes take children as young as five or six. You can use the camp's enrollment age range as one guide to deciding when the time is right for overnight camp. Most camps set this range based on their actual experience with boys and girls of different ages. For example, if the camp enrolls a sizeable group of eight-year-olds, then that camp probably has had good luck with most kids that age.

For camps that offer only one long session, you should consider your child's age and experience as well as the camp's visiting policy. Generally speaking, younger kids, with little previous experience away from home, prefer sessions shorter than six weeks if it's their first time away at camp. However, a session that lasts six weeks or more probably includes several family visiting days. Some of these full-summer camps enroll children as young as seven, but allow parents to visit any time after the first two weeks. However, enrolling for the first time in a full-summer camp should be a thoughtful decision, regardless of the visiting policy. In fact, camps that last all summer will often interview prospective campers and their parents before enrolling them. The staff know that every child's love of camp and tolerance for separations is different, and the interviews help ensure a good fit between the child and the camp.

We believe that two weeks is the shortest camp session that can provide children with a true sense of belonging and a fair measure of independence. One week can certainly be fun, but it may not be long enough for children to develop the friendships and familiarity necessary to accomplish any of the goals of overnight camping besides Goal 1: Have fun. If it's your child's first time away from home, and if she's not interested in a two-week camp, then by all means consider a camp with a shorter session. The important thing is that she enjoys her first time at overnight camp.

What else should parents consider?

Besides your child's level of interest, age, and the length of each camp session, there are four other factors to consider when deciding whether the time is right for overnight camp: experience, attitude, family, and parents.

Experience

It has been said that experience is the best teacher. This is certainly true of overnight camping. Some practice time away from home will give your child an idea of whether the time is right for a session of overnight camp. This preliminary experience could be a sleep-over or a long weekend at a friend's house, a week alone with relatives, a two-day school trip, or an overnight Scout or youth group outing. Here is one boy's opinion about what makes it easier for older children to leave home and spend time at overnight camp:

> I think that older kids have gone away on school trips, like on a skiing trip, and they know how it is to be, like, away from your parents and they're more mature . . . they can use breaks from their parents. . . . When you spend time away from home, you learn that you're not with your parents, but you'll always be in their mind and stuff. It gets easier and easier to spend time away from home. — Bobby, age 9

Our research suggests that boys and girls with some previous experience being away from home are generally less likely to be homesick than children who have never spent any time away from home. It's just as nine-year-old Bobby observed. Indeed, most children have an intuitive feeling about when they are ready to be away from home, and how long seems comfortable. Talking with your child about these feelings will make it easier to decide on the best time to go to camp, the best camp to attend, and the best length of stay.

Attitude

Your child's attitude about living at overnight camp is another important factor to consider. In several studies, we found that boys and girls who had positive expectations about camp had more fun and were generally less homesick than children who thought camp was going to stink. This makes sense. One way to help your child develop a positive attitude about camp is to include him in decisions about camp. Let him help you decide when to go away to camp, how long to stay, and which camp is best. Also, learn as much as possible about the camp you choose before you send him. Just like adults, kids feel less apprehensive when they know what's going to happen, where it's going to happen, and what's expected of them. They develop positive attitudes about their camp when it feels familiar.

Family

Families are constantly changing. New babies are born. Grandparents die. Friends move away. Parents get separated or divorced. Kids change schools. Cousins come to stay for a while. All sorts of things can happen to a family. Many of the changes are joyous. Other changes are stressful and sad.

To a child, going away to overnight camp can be happy, stressful, and sad all at once. Therefore, when you think about whether the time is right for your child, you must think about whether the *timing* is right for the whole family. Our studies have demonstrated that stressful family events do not necessarily make it harder for children to have fun at camp. Stressful separations, like the death or illness of a loved one, divorce, custody changes, or a move to a new house, may or may not make the separation from home difficult for your child. It really varies from one child to another.

So how will you know whether your child can adjust to overnight camp after a recent stressful family event? There's no way to tell for sure, but talking about the transition to camp with your child is a good place to start. It's normal for kids (and parents, too!) to be nervous about overnight camp if the family has recently suffered a loss. For all the wonderful independence that overnight camp instills in children, there are times when a family needs to be all together. If your child is excessively worried about leaving home, or if she's unusually depressed, clingy, or upset, you should talk with her about the possibility of not going away to overnight camp this year. There will always be next year.

Remember, your child's attitude about camp is a good predictor of whether she'll have a fun time or not. It's hard for kids to have fun at camp when they are worried about things that are happening at home. Therefore, avoid using camp as a place to sequester your child during a period of transition or loss. Instead of insulating her from stress, you might just be giving her the time and space to ruminate. On the other hand, if your family has had enough time to deal with a recent stressful event, and your child is enthusiastic about overnight camp, then camp might be the perfect thing for both of you.

Parents

It's important to consider your own attitudes and behaviors because they influence your child's attitudes and behaviors. If you're nervous about his going away to camp, it will show, no matter how hard you try to hide it. Of course, a little bit of nervousness is OK. It's perfectly normal for parents to be a little sad and nervous when their child goes away, and kids know that. But if you show a great deal of sadness or anxiety, then your child may think to himself, "Gee, if my parents are that upset about the whole camp thing, then there must be something scary about it. I should probably be pretty upset too." The research findings won't surprise you. Children who are very nervous or sad in the months before they come to camp are more likely to feel nervous, sad, and homesick at camp than children who are relatively cheerful in the months prior to camp.

There is one other reason to monitor your own attitudes and behaviors. If you seem very distressed, then your child might feel guilty

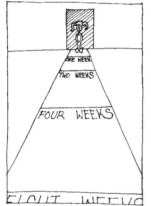

about leaving home. The principle is simple: If your child is worried about you, it is harder for him to concentrate on having fun at camp. He might feel that his job should be to stay home and take care of you. You may need to assure him that you'll be fine, and that you'll have a lot to do while he's away at camp.

Despite giving your child uniformly positive messages about camp, you may nevertheless find her getting cold feet just prior to opening day. This is common for first-year campers, but even veteran campers get nervous about whether their old friends will be back, what might have changed about camp, and who their cabin leader will be. Some kids may become quite upset and adamant about withdrawing their enrollment at the last minute, and parents struggle not to cave in to these emotional demands. In such cases, it's important to be empathetic but committed. So far, you've been collaborating with your child about her decision to go to camp. A day or two before camp starts, however, is a time to be firm and confident. You might say something like, "Madeline, I know how excited you are for camp to start, but I can see that part of you is nervous now that opening day is almost here. It's normal to be wondering what camp will be like, but once you get to camp, you'll be able to answer a lot of the questions you have now. I'm glad we've made a careful decision about camp together, and we both know it'll be wonderful. I want you to go and have a good time. I know it can hurt a little to leave home, but once you get into the routine at camp, you'll love it. Don't forget: We'll be in touch, so you can tell me how you're doing." Your child is likely to appreciate your unwavering vote of loving confidence.

Checklist

❑ Consider your child's level of interest in overnight camp. What sparked her interest? Has her interest endured, or have you had to do a lot of convincing? If your child goes to camp, will she be going for herself or for you?

❑ Consider your child's age. Children younger than 7 may have a difficult time adjusting to a week or more of overnight camp. Is he ready?

❑ Consider the length of stay that is best. How many weeks are best for you, your child, and the family? Are there adequate visiting days? How will camp fit in with the rest of your summer plans?

❑ Consider your child's previous experiences away from home. Has he spent at least a few weekends away from home? What were those separations like for him and for you?

❑ Consider your child's attitude toward camp. Is she excited or does she think that camp will stink? Sometimes attitudes become self-fulfilling prophecies, so do your best to create positive expectations. Learn as much as you can about the camp you eventually choose.

❑ Consider your family situation. Have there been recent stressful changes within the family? Have there been losses or unexpected separations? Have you and your child adjusted to those changes? Are you both ready to be apart from each other?

❑ Consider your own approach to camp. Encouragement is important, but check to make sure you're not being too pushy early on. Also, it's normal to be nervous, but check to make sure you're not doing too much worrying out loud.

❑ Be sure you send a clear message that camp is a good thing and that you'll both enjoy the time apart. Avoid sending mixed messages. Be firm and confident as opening day nears.

P.S. You work hard as a parent, and you deserve some time off. You should feel good about providing a wonderful experience for your child, and giving yourself a well-earned break from full-time parenthood.

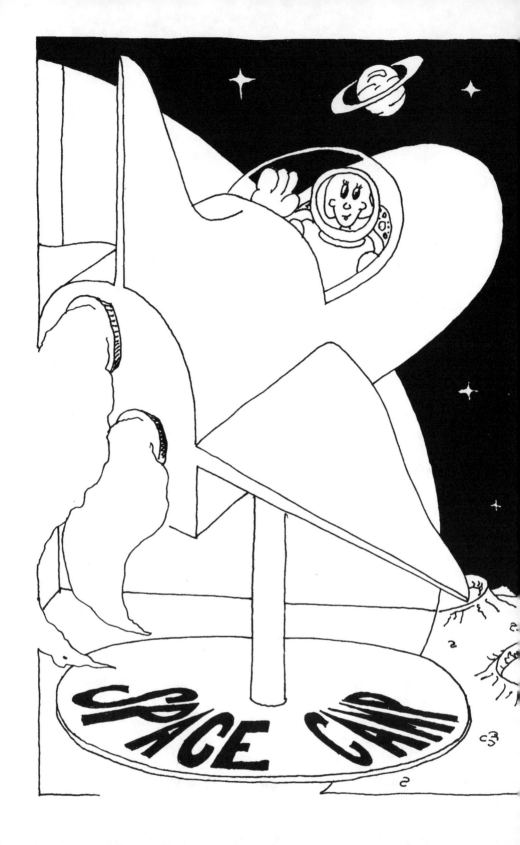

CHAPTER 4

Different types of overnight camps

Just imagine horseback riding through a country field, joking around with seven of your best friends, shooting baskets in the sunshine, reading in the shade of a big oak tree, sailing across a clear blue lake, silk-screening your own T-shirt design, starring in a play, scoring a goal for your street hockey team, scaling a rock wall, playing volleyball on the beach with your cabin mates, or carving it up on a snowboarding trail. All of these things are possible at different overnight camps across the country. Yet how can you possibly choose from among the nearly 6,300 overnight camps in the United States? Well, after you and your child have imagined what he'd like best, you'll want to discuss the different types of camps that are available.

Before selecting a specific camp, you should know that there are three general types of overnight camps: traditional, specialty, and special needs. Your goal for this chapter should be to figure out what type of camp is right for your child in terms of content, atmosphere, and setting. Then you'll be ready to start the selection process.

Traditional overnight camps

What separates traditional overnight camps from specialty camps and special needs camps is the tremendous variety of activities. This variety is not only the spice of life; it's also the best way to make sure everyone has a good time. Nearly every activity will be some camper's favorite.

Most traditional camps offer more than 50 different athletic and artistic activities. For example, two traditional camps we know (one for boys and one for girls) offer the following activities every day: swimming, canoeing, sailing, sailboarding, water-skiing, rowing, soccer, lacrosse, basketball, baseball, kickball, softball, football, tennis, Frisbee-golf, archery, riflery, nature education, arts and crafts, drama, street hockey, volleyball, camp craft, horseshoes, low ropes course, whiffleball, hiking, ping-pong, tetherball, mini-golf, music, horseback riding, and photography.

In addition to these conventional activities, every traditional camp also has some original games and special activities. Some traditional camps have things like a library, non-denominational vespers services, weekly campfires, intercamp teams, and invented sports that defy description, such as *Bizou Ball* and *The Blob*. As the name implies, traditional camps also have their own set of traditional games, songs, stories, and ceremonies. These time-honored elements add character to an environment that otherwise might seem generic, and they promote a strong sense of community. Year after year, campers and staff feel part of something special.

Most traditional overnight camps have their own rural campus with permanent buildings, activity facilities (such as courts, fields, and docks), and a full-time staff. Living quarters range from small canvas tents to cabins with electricity and plumbing. Bedding can range from sleeping bags to wooden beds with mattresses, fitted sheets, and blankets. Campers usually eat meals in large dining halls. Food is served either cafeteria style, where each child moves through a line and puts her food on a tray before joining other campers at a table, or family style, where groups of children sit together and fill their plates from platters of food that the whole table shares.

Many traditional overnight camps have existed for generations. A handful are still going strong 100 years or more after they began. Some traditional camps are known as *agency camps*. These camps are sponsored or run by venerable organizations, such as the Scouts, the YMCA, Camp Fire Boys and Girls, and various churches and synagogues. There are also many traditional overnight camps that are privately owned family businesses. A few are run by private corporations. Regardless of the sponsorship, most people's typical mental picture of summer camp fits into the traditional overnight camp category.

Pros and Cons of Traditional Overnight Camps

Pros include:

- A tremendous variety of fun individual and group activities
- Many chances to try new things, experiment, and be creative
- An emphasis on outdoor activities and living in harmony with nature
- Traditional games, songs, stories, and ceremonies
- Opportunities to build individual character as well as a strong sense of community
- Cabin leaders are usually trained in leadership skills

Cons include:

- Fewer opportunities to specialize in one particular activity (compared to a specialty camp)
- Cabin leaders may be generalists, not expert instructors in their field
- Fewer accommodations for special needs (compared to a special needs camp)
- Fewer chances to work on academic activities (compared to an academic specialty camp)

Specialty overnight camps

Whereas traditional camps flourish with a broad range of activity offerings and a general emphasis on character building, the strength of specialty camps is their narrow, concentrated set of activity offerings. Specialty camps include sports, trips, arts, and academic camps.

Sports Camp

The competitive nature of our society and the specialized interest of many kids has sustained a new kind of overnight camp: the sports camp. These camps focus on a single sport, such as soccer, basketball, sailing, or tennis. Some of these camps are associated with famous athletes. They have names like, Walter Percival Football Camp and Evelyn Swanson Tennis Camp. Others are sponsored by regional, national, or corporate sports associations, such as Nike® Tennis Camp. If your child is crazy about a particular sport, a specialty sports camp may be just the thing.

Developing mastery in a particular sport can give your child a gratifying sense of competence and a better chance at making school teams.

The daily schedule at sports camps tends to include large blocks of time, in both the morning and afternoon, dedicated to improving skills in the specialty sport. Evening specialty sessions are also common, but good specialty sports camps add variety to the daily schedule so that campers don't get bored. Some time is almost always devoted to non-specialty activities, such as other sports, games, or free time. Non-specialty program periods may also include activities related to the specialty sport, such as watching game films or meeting a sports celebrity.

Specialty sports camps are set up in a variety of locations. Some are in woodsy, rural, outdoor settings just like most traditional overnight camps. There, you might expect the same range of living and dining facilities. Other specialty sports camps are situated on college campuses in order to take advantage of specialized equipment and facilities, such as gymnasiums and stadiums. At these camps, kids usually live in a dormitory and eat meals in a cafeteria.

A college campus may offer excellent facilities, but the leadership and supervision that staff can provide may be compromised by two factors. First, a college campus is not as enclosed as a rural camp. Therefore, close supervision of each child is more difficult. Young campers may wander into town without realizing they have left the campus or gone out of bounds. Second, a college campus usually has non-camp people coming and going, even during the summer. Some of them may not provide the good examples that well-trained cabin leaders do. Obviously, the wholesomeness of the setting is an important factor to consider when choosing any overnight camp.

Travel and Trip Camp

True travel and trip camps specialize in exploring geographic and topographic places of interest. Often, groups of children travel by car, bus, or plane to a base camp or main lodge where they learn about wilderness camping and the modes of transportation they will be using. These may range from hiking and backpacking to canoeing and sea kayaking; from snow-shoeing to horseback riding. There are even caravan camps that travel many miles in covered wagons.

At a trip camp, groups of children and trip leaders may be off for weeks at a time in uncharted wilderness, or they may frequent campsites in national and state parks. They may even follow famous routes, such as

the Appalachian Trail, which stretches along the eastern United States from Georgia to Maine. In general, travel and trip camps are the most outdoorsy and rugged of any type of camp, specialty or otherwise. Their power to challenge and inspire kids is unique. Older adolescents and young adults who like these aspects of travel and trip camps may eventually wish to try adventure and leadership schools, such as Outward Bound and the National Outdoor Leadership School.

Fine Arts/Performing Arts Camp

Fine arts camps offer specialized instruction in a variety of media such as painting, sculpture, photography, film and video, printing, writing, and various crafts. Performing arts camps specialize in theater, dance, and music. Many also offer a selection of other activities. At a typical arts specialty camp, your child might spend the better part of each day practicing an instrument, learning a specific art or craft, or working on the production of a play. Activities include lessons, practices, workshops, performances, exhibits, productions, training exercises, and improvisation. The combination of specialized work in an art form and community living with other young artists and performers is energizing.

The facilities at an arts specialty camp are specific to the discipline in question. At music camps, there are usually practice rooms and concert halls with good acoustics. At fine arts camps, there may be specialized pieces of equipment, such as kilns, woodworking tools, and easels. At theater camps, there are probably stages, lighting equipment, and costumes. Although many traditional camps offer musical, artistic, and theatrical activities, the facilities and instruction at a fine arts specialty camp are generally superior. The more serious your child is about his art form, the more important it will be to verify that the camp you choose has the kind of equipment, facilities, and instructors that will meet his needs.

Most arts camps have performances or exhibits at the end of the session. If you are interested in an arts specialty camp, be sure to find out how the performances or exhibits are produced. Does every child get a chance to participate? Are performances or exhibits open to parents and friends? If not, are they videotaped? Is the philosophy of the camp inclusive or competitive? Are there opportunities for kids at all skill levels, or only expert?

Like specialty sports camps, arts specialty camps are set up in a variety of locations. Different locations offer different living and dining facilities. Some young performers and artists feel inspired in natural, outdoor settings; others feel distracted. Consider the advantages and disadvantages of the setting, as well as the instructors' expertise, when choosing an arts specialty camp.

Academic or Technical Camp

Like other kinds of specialty camps, these camps offer specialized programs, often on college campuses. Campers spend a considerable amount of time honing their skills in one or more academic or technical subjects. The classic academic camp is a foreign language camp. These camps include a week or more of linguistic and cultural immersion, coupled with a traditional program of outdoor activities. Lately, computer camps, space camps, and broadcasting camps have grown in popularity because of technological advances in those areas.

No matter what academic or technical subject you and your child seek, from philosophy to engineering to SAT preparation, you can probably find a specialty overnight camp to match. Academic or technical specialty camps are great ways for kids to expand their intellectual horizons without the normal pressures of school, such as grades and dress codes. Academic and technical specialty camps may also provide better equipment, better instruction, and fewer distractions than your child's school.

Some academic or technical specialty camps are intended for kids who need extra help in a particular area. These are called *remedial* camps or sometimes *camp schools*. Don't confuse this with *summer school*, which is simply going to school in the summer. Other academic or technical specialty camps are designed for advanced, accelerated, or gifted students. At any academic or technical specialty camp, there is always the possibility that kids won't develop their social and athletic skills much. However, these skills are important too, and the directors of high quality academic and technical specialty camps know that. No matter how sophisticated the instruction, these specialty camps should also include plenty of time each day for kids to do activities outside their academic or technical realm.

Like the other kinds of specialty camps we've discussed, specialty academic or technical camps are set up in a variety of locations. However, the more electronic and computerized the specialty, the less likely the camp is to be located in a beautiful, natural, outdoor setting. Because good old fashioned fresh air is so beneficial, we again recommend that you carefully consider the setting, not just the sophistication of the equipment, when choosing an academic or technical specialty camp. Some kids like to get the best of both worlds. Their parents arrange a week at an urban academic or technical specialty camp followed by a couple of weeks at a traditional, rural, outdoor overnight camp. Parents we know who have arranged this combination point out that when kids spend time on an academic campus, they get a chance to see what college is like, and maybe even get excited about going. Clearly, every location has its perks.

A note about fancy electronic equipment: Remember that it can all break down. Parents and kids should ask: Will there be anything at all to do at this camp if the power goes out? Are there enough machines for everyone? How many times does each kid actually get to ride in the space shuttle simulator? Beware of an academic or technical specialty camp that seems to use one impressive piece of equipment as its sole selling point. Any high quality camp, whether traditional or specialty, should offer a variety of activities. Any high quality camp should also have back-up plans and rainy-day activities for times when equipment is down or unusable.

Pros and Cons of Specialty Overnight Camps

Pros include:

- Immersion in a favorite sport, art form, language, or academic subject
- Improving skills in a preferred specialty
- Opportunities to earn nationally recognized certification in a particular specialty, such as SCUBA, sailing, or computer programming
- The chance to hang out with kids who share much in common
- Working with instructors who are experts, perhaps even celebrities, in their specialty

Cons include:

- Doing mostly one activity for a week or more may get tiresome.
- Instruction in activities besides the specialty may not be excellent.
- Some specialty camp locations, such as college campuses, may not offer the outdoor experience, close supervision, and quality leadership that traditional camps do.
- Celebrities at celebrity sports camps may not actually work at the camp each day.
- Expert instructors are not necessarily trained in leadership skills.

Special needs overnight camps

Special needs overnight camps fall into three basic categories, based on the needs of the child: physical, psychological, and weight loss. All three kinds strive to boost children's self-esteem and improve their coping skills by providing a safe, supportive environment where children with similar needs can share their experience and learn from staff and one another. Such camps also strive to teach kids healthy habits. For example, kids at a diabetes camp learn new ways of controlling their blood sugar through diet, exercise, and proper insulin dosing. The best part of any special needs overnight camp is that children learn to do new things, including some they never thought they could. A supportive, beautiful camp environment is the perfect place for kids to test the limits of their abilities.

It makes intuitive sense that kids with special needs would benefit from overnight camp. The experience of community living away from home, with other kids who have similar needs, and with adult staff who are trained to help kids deal with their special needs, can be incredibly powerful. Imagine what an extremely positive experience it is for a child who has survived the pain and disfigurement of a severe burn to spend a week or more with other children who have survived the same trauma. Or, imagine how much a child with leukemia can learn about coping with his disease when he spends a few weeks at overnight camp with other children who are fighting cancer. Not surprisingly, recent research has confirmed that special needs camps often boost children's self-esteem and improve their coping skills.

A few special needs camps take place on college campuses or even in hospitals. However, most special needs camps take place in natural, outdoor settings, typical of traditional overnight camps. Indeed, many special needs camps exist by renting the campus of a traditional overnight camp for a week or two. This works out well, as long as the special needs camp staff who comes in to run things is highly qualified and familiar with the camp grounds.

The physical and mental health care staff at any special needs camp should be qualified to care for the specific needs of the children they serve. For example, the nurse at a camp for kids with asthma should have expertise using nebulizers (special machines that administer asthma medicines). The doctor affiliated with a camp for diabetic children should be an endocrinologist (a doctor who specializes in the care of diabetes). The nutritionist at a weight-loss camp should be qualified to work with children and teens. The psychologist or psychiatrist at a camp for kids with attention deficit hyperactivity disorder or severe behavior problems should have lots of experience managing children's emotional and behavioral difficulties.

Special needs camps should also be designed for the kids they serve. Ramps and rails must be provided for those who use wheelchairs. Staff-to-camper ratios must be higher to allow for the individual attention that some kids with special needs require. Special medical equipment must be readily available if required. Above all, the staff should be highly trained in helping kids manage their specific needs. It's not enough for the staff to be a group of untrained people who are simply interested in helping children. That's a good start, but specialized leadership and health care training is necessary. Without it, staff at overnight camps for kids with special needs may provide inadequate or inappropriate supervision.

Camping programs are available for kids who have a variety of special needs, including the following:

- arthritis
- asthma/respiratory ailments
- attention deficit hyperactivity disorder
- autism, Asperger's disorder, or pervasive developmental disorder
- blindness/visual impairment
- burns
- cancer

- cerebral palsy
- cystic fibrosis
- deafness/hearing impairment
- diabetes
- epilepsy/seizure disorder
- hemophilia
- HIV/AIDS
- kidney disorders
- mental retardation
- mobility limitations/amputations/other physical disabilities
- muscular dystrophy
- multiple sclerosis
- obesity
- severe behavior problems
- sickle cell anemia
- spina bifida
- spinal injury or paralysis
- substance abuse

Many special needs camps offer sessions that run for several weeks, as traditional camps do. Shorter stays are also common. Whatever the length of stay, spending time at special needs overnight camp can be a wonderful experience for kids and will provide well-deserved respite for parents. Special needs overnight camps are also available for older adolescents and adults with disabilities. You can start your research on special needs camps (and traditional camps that have inclusion programs) by talking with one or more of the health care professionals who cares for your child. Next, look in *Resources & references* at the end of this book for more information on electronic and printed material about special needs camps.

Weight-loss camps deserve additional discussion because millions of American kids struggle with their weight and because weight-loss camps are increasingly popular. These camps are designed to boost kids' self-esteem and instill exercise and diet habits that they can bring home. Some kids succeed at weight-loss camps and feel great about how their bodies change. Naturally, other kids fail to meet or maintain their weight-loss goals. As with other kinds of specialty overnight camps, you'll want to research the philosophy and design of the camp and then decide whether it offers something new and potentially helpful to your child. As a consumer, you should know that weight-loss camps, like certain weight-loss products, may make dramatic claims about how much weight a child can lose during a camp stay.

It's uncommon, but attending a special needs camp might foster labeling or even ridicule. Kids may call weight-loss camps "fat farms," or they may label campers who attend military-style camps "jeuvies," "delinquents," or "burn-outs." Kids can be cruel to one another, purely out of ignorance. Boys and girls who attend weight-loss camps may be especially vulnerable to labeling because obesity is such a stigma in modern society. Of course, if the camp helps your child meet his goals, the opportunity for teasing will disappear along with the excess weight.

As an alternative to attending a special needs camp, you and your child may wish to consider traditional camps that make accommodations for special needs. More and more traditional camps have inclusion programs and specially trained staff for this purpose. These camps provide wonderful experiences and may reduce the likelihood of labeling because they are seen as "normal" camps.

Pros and Cons of Special Needs Overnight Camps

Pros include:

- Opportunities to improve coping with special physical, psychological, or weight-loss needs
- The chance to befriend and learn from kids who face similar challenges
- Feeling supported and safe in an environment where all the other kids face similar challenges
- Staff who are experienced in helping kids manage their special needs

Cons include:

- Staff may know a lot about the special need, or really want to help kids with special needs, but they may know little about leadership or instruction.

- Rented camp grounds may belong to an accredited camp, but the special needs camp may not be run according to recognized camping standards.

- Living exclusively with other children who have special needs may get tiresome, depressing, or even upsetting.

Religion and spirituality

All overnight camps exist along a spectrum of religiosity, from highly religious to non-religious. How can you tell where a camp lies on this spectrum? First, determine what sort of organization, if any, sponsors the camp. If the sponsor is an orthodox, conservative, or evangelical organization, camp life probably has a heavy dose of religion. It might even be considered a religious specialty camp. At such a camp, your child may feel like an outsider if she is not of the same faith as her cabin mates.

Next, find out what proportion of the staff and campers identify themselves with a particular faith and how religion fits into the daily program of activities. Some camps have a religiously homogeneous staff and a considerable amount of worship and scripture study built into the daily program. Other camps, with diverse staffs and only a few religious practices, are closer to the middle of the religiosity spectrum. Naturally, if there is no mention of religion whatsoever, probably the camp is completely non-religious.

At first glance, it may seem as if many traditional camps are moderately or highly religious because they have important spiritual components to their program. These can include a secular or religious daily vespers service, some kind of weekend service, or mealtime prayers. At many traditional camps, these spiritual components are important parts of the camp's program and traditions, but they are not the focus of each camp day, nor are they the camp's major selling point. By contrast, highly religious camps clearly emphasize that a major part of each camp day includes divine worship and holy scripture study.

In addition to formal worship and study, highly religious camps integrate religious themes into everyday games, songs, stories, and sports. The campers may be required to conform to certain diets, activities, and codes of dress and behavior. Staff members are usually carefully selected according to their religious beliefs. Such camps give children an unparalleled opportunity to grow spiritually in the company of other children and adult role models who share their faith. Most highly religious camps are designed to serve children whose families are members of a particular religious group or members of a specific church, synagogue, temple, or mosque.

Some religiously affiliated camps, such as those sponsored by the YMCA (Young Men's Christian Association), are less religious than you might think. Despite its roots in Protestant Christian social movements of the late nineteenth century, the YMCA today has adopted the following inclusive mission statement:

> To put Christian principles into practice through programs that build healthy spirit, mind, and body for all.

You might be surprised to learn that a large number of YMCA camps have sizable Jewish, Catholic, and agnostic campers and staffs. For example, at one YMCA camp we know, about 25% of the campers and staff are Jewish. They feel perfectly comfortable with the camp's Judeo-Christian value system and non-denominational vespers.

Here's what some Jewish parents and children have to say about their experiences with YMCA overnight camps. Their experiences may not be typical, but they illustrate the inclusive nature of the YMCA's mission, as well as the potential weakness of a broad religious affiliation.

> *Even though our family is Jewish, I felt perfectly comfortable sending Eric to a YMCA camp. Few people perceive the YMCA as a religious organization anymore. It's more about caring for one another.* —Eric's mom, Ellen

> *Jews have always assimilated; they still have to. So sending Scott to a Y camp wasn't a compromise. I called ahead to find out how much religion was in the camp program and what the demographics of the camp population were. I felt perfectly comfortable sending him to a Y camp because the values and services were Judeo-Christian, as advertised.* —Scott's dad, Sheldon

> *In our community, there aren't many Jewish kids, so it was important to me to send my son to a Jewish camp. YMCA camps may teach Judeo-Christian principles, but to instill Judaism, we chose a strongly religious, Jewish camp.*
> —Joel's mom, Elcha

> *I thought I was going to be the only Jewish kid at an all-Christian camp, but there turned out to be a lot of other Jewish kids here. I guess if I were Orthodox, I wouldn't like it here, because the food isn't kosher. But none of*

the kids here are Orthodox anything—Christian or Jew. Everybody lives together in peace here.   —Shoshana, age 16

Even though I'm Jewish, the cross in the chapel doesn't bother me. It's there; it stands for something, but no one shoves religion down our throats here. I don't even know what religion most of the campers and leaders here are, but they're all nice. That's what's important to me. I can go to temple at home.
                                                    —Gary, third-year cabin leader

Although young people of all faiths are welcomed at YMCA camps, some of these camps are more religious than others. The same could be said of camps that belong to the Young Men's Hebrew Association or the Association of Jewish Sponsored Camps. Call the director if you have questions about where a camp lies on the religiosity spectrum.

When you look at a camp, in person or in pictures, remember that facilities such as outdoor chapels do not necessarily mean that the camp is a religious specialty camp. Most traditional camps founded in a Christian tradition still have chapels for Sunday services and daily vespers. However, services at these camps are usually delivered by staff from all faiths. As opposed to being a time of formal religious worship, these services have evolved into a time for staff to share ideas, tell stories with a moral, or describe personal philosophies.

As you learn about individual camps, note your comfort with their religious intensity. Whatever type of camp you're looking for, you can probably find highly religious and non-religious versions. If you want something in between—some type of non-denominational worship—but you're not comfortable with a highly religious camp, consider a religiously-affiliated camp that can accommodate your child's religious needs, such as a kosher diet, a weekly trip to Sunday services, or a time for prayer. Remember, too, that organized religion is just one manifestation of spirituality. A camp can be spiritual, by promoting a sense of peace, friendship, community, and closeness to nature, without having any overtly religious elements.

Checklist

We are most interested in:

- ❏ Traditional overnight camp
- ❏ Specialty overnight camp
- ❏ Special needs camp
- ❏ Dividing time between two different types of camps

The setting that we like best is:

- ❏ Rugged wilderness
- ❏ Rural, woodsy, and outdoors
- ❏ Urban and mostly indoors
- ❏ A college or university campus

The religious and spiritual atmosphere we prefer is:

- ❏ Highly religious
- ❏ Moderately religious
- ❏ Spiritual but non-denominational
- ❏ Non-religious

PART II

SELECTING
A CAMP

CHAPTER 5

Step 1: Focus your search

After reading Chapter 4, you should know what type of overnight camp you and your son or daughter are looking for. In this chapter, we'll help you focus your search. Below is the checklist for this chapter. It summarizes the basic choices you need to make. Skim it now, so you know what's ahead. Then, as you read, turn back to the checklist and make your decisions. You may wish to make your own, additional notes.

Checklist
Where do you want to go to camp?

- ❏ Close to home
- ❏ Far from home
- ❏ Far from our home, but close to a family friend or relative's home

How long do you want to stay at camp?

- ❑ Less than one week
- ❑ One week
- ❑ Two weeks
- ❑ Three or four weeks
- ❑ More than four weeks
- ❑ A week or more at a few different camps

Do you want a single-sex or coed camp? What type?

- ❑ All boys, with no girls' camps on the property
- ❑ All boys, with a sister camp on the same property
- ❑ All girls, with no boys' camps on the property
- ❑ All girls, with a brother camp on the same property
- ❑ Coed, where boys and girls do program activities and dine together
- ❑ Coed, where boys and girls do program activities separately, but dine together

What kind of organization do you want?

Living Quarters

- ❑ Children of similar ages or grades live together
- ❑ Children of different ages and grades live together

Staffing of Living Quarters

- ❑ Cabin leaders live with campers
- ❑ Supervising adults live nearby, but no adult lives with campers

Activity Periods

- ❑ Maximum structure, where staff schedule most things for campers
- ❑ Almost complete freedom, where campers choose what to do and when to do it
- ❑ A balance of choices and structured time

Getting started

There are four basic questions that you need to answer before you start gathering specific information about overnight camps. If you don't answer these questions first, you'll end up with a pile of camp brochures and videos so huge that you'll need binoculars to see the top.

The questions are:

1. Where do you want to go to camp?

2. How long do you want to stay?

3. Do you want a single-sex or coed camp?

4. What kind of organization do you want?

We'll discuss each one of these topics in turn.

1. Where do you want to go to camp?

You've got to pick a geographic region before you start gathering information about specific camps. Would you and your child prefer a camp close to home, far from home, or far from home but close to family? Each choice has advantages. You should also consider the unique advantages of certain geographical locations.

Close to Home

Some families pick a camp close to home. The advantages of going to overnight camp close to home are:

- You may have an easier time visiting the camp to evaluate it before you go.
- You can find families near you, whose children attended that camp, who can give you helpful first-hand information.
- It's less expensive to travel there than to a faraway camp.
- If the camp is in your home state, there may be an in-state tuition discount.
- Your child may have cabin mates from your home town or school.
- Letters will take only a couple of days to get back and forth to camp.
- On visiting days and closing days, parents will have an easier time getting to camp.

You might think that going to an overnight camp close to home reduces the chance of strong homesick feelings. Surprisingly, that's not the case for most kids. The number of miles kids travel away from home has almost nothing to do with how much fun they have at camp. Boys and girls who live 7 miles from camp are as likely to feel homesick as those who live 70 or 700 or even 7000 miles from camp. Being geographically close to home does not make the adjustment to camp any easier or harder. It depends instead on the individual child's experience and attitude, her family situation, and the camp.

Far from Home

Some families pick a camp that is far from home. The advantages of going to a camp far from home are:

- It will give you more choices when choosing a camp.
- Many kids, especially teens, enjoy making long trips on their own.
- It may provide a completely different environment. Depending on where you live, this change in environment could mean big mountains, a lake, snow, warm weather, the ocean, or even a country where English is not the primary language.
- There's a chance that some of the other kids at camp will be pretty different from your child, which adds some diversity to the experience.
- It may provide an excuse for parents to join their children when camp is over, and add a family vacation to the summer plans.

Far from Home but Close to Family

Being close to home or far from home are not the only two options. You can also choose a camp that is far from your home, but close to a relative's home. For some families, this option is the best of both worlds. You can have all the advantages of going to a faraway camp, but still have the security and convenience of a nearby camp. Some West Coast parents we know send their children to camps on the East Coast, but they chose a camp that is near the grandparents' house. Typically, the grandparents will pick up the child at the airport and drive him to camp. Of course, it doesn't have to be grandparents. Any close friend or relative might be able to help your child feel comfortable going to a distant camp. If yours is one of the rare families who has a second home in a different part of the

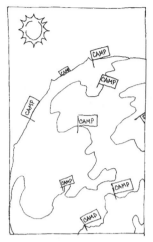

country, then you may want to look at camps near that second home.

Geographic Location

In addition to distance from home and proximity to family, you should consider the unique advantages of certain geographic locations. Certain settings are better suited for certain activities than others. For example, if your child is interested primarily in snorkeling or SCUBA diving, you'll want to look at camps on the southwest and southeast coasts. If your child is interested primarily in skiing or snowboarding, you'll want to check out camps in the Rocky Mountains. Although most campgrounds are varied enough to accommodate a wide range of activities, your choice of a geographic location should take into account the region's special features. Consider the climate, landscape, and bodies of water that your child needs to do the activities she likes, and factor these into your choice of a geographic location. If your finances permit, consider the unique geography of camps outside the United States.

2. How long do you want to stay at camp?

At this point, you and your child need not decide exactly how many days or weeks to spend at camp. However, you should both think about what range seems best. A week or less? Two weeks? A month or more? As we discussed in Chapter 3, short sessions may be best for first-time campers, and long sessions build deep friendships. However, your child can have fun, learn new skills, develop independence, make friends, and experience a new environment no matter how long the session lasts. Much of your decision rests on your personal comfort level and your finances.

Start by asking your child what length of stay he prefers. To help find the answer, compare the choices you offer to other events that have lasted for the same amount of time. For example, you might ask, "How does a two-week session sound? That's how long winter vacation lasted. Does that seem like too long or too short for overnight camp?" Or, you might ask, "How does a week at camp sound? That's how long you went to visit

Uncle Mike and Aunt Jessie last summer. How would that be?" Kids need these concrete examples to get a feel for how long a certain time period is. Without examples, young children have an especially hard time imagining what a week or a month actually feels like.

The longer the length of stay you choose, the more important it becomes to select a camp that has a well-rounded program. If the camp repeats the same program week after week, or if it's a specialty camp with a narrow range of activities, long stays may become boring. Years ago, almost every traditional overnight camp lasted the whole summer. If your grandparents went to overnight camp, there's a good chance they stayed for six or eight weeks. That may seem like a long time to be away from home, especially if it's your first time. However, camps that offer long sessions usually have excellent, progressive, well-rounded programs with many different activity choices and multiple visiting days. One advantage to a long length of stay at a well-designed camp is that campers can achieve tremendous skill levels in whatever activities they choose. For example, you simply cannot go through all the archery or riflery marksmanship rankings, learn the finer points of English riding, or become an expert sailor in one short week. Those sorts of accomplishments require a longer session.

There's one more issue to consider regarding length of stay. Consecutive short stays can get complicated. For example, it's usually easier for families to work out one three-week stay at a camp than it is to work out three consecutive one-week stays at three different camps. If your child is excited about spending three weeks away from home, then try to find one camp that offers a three-week session. There are several disadvantages to attending a bunch of short-stay camps:

- Multiple camp stays are usually more expensive, in both tuition and travel, than a single camp stay of the same total length.

- Unpacking and re-packing between each camp gets to be a hassle.

- Adjusting to a new group of friends is not easy, especially when kids have to do it three or four times in a row in three or four different environments.

- It's hard for kids to make an emotional commitment to one camp when they know they'll be leaving soon for another camp.

Some parents and children do schedule two or three different camps each summer, especially if one of the camps is a specialty camp. This is a great option for some kids, and many families manage to work out the details successfully. Our advice is simply to think carefully before you schedule several camps back-to-back. Variety is good, but a cramped schedule isn't.

3. Do you want a single-sex or coed camp?

For most campers and staff, a single-sex environment offers fewer romantic distractions. It's a bit easier for everyone to focus on the goals of overnight camp that we discussed in Chapter 2. There tends to be less showing off, reduced self-consciousness, and fewer broken hearts. At a single-sex camp, children support each other and bond together in ways that reinforce the best parts about being a girl or the best parts about being a boy. Plus, the staff at a single-sex camp is primarily the same sex as the campers. This provides kids with many adult role models of the same gender. These role models can help kids escape unhealthy cultural stereotypes of what is masculine and what is feminine. Girls' inner voices stay strong and alive, and boys are not pressured to disconnect from relationships.

Single-sex overnight camps have unique advantages. However, one of the goals of overnight camping is to make friends and develop social skills. If your child attends a single-sex private school from September to June, then a coed summer camp may be the perfect way to balance his peer group and round-out his social skills. Remember that one of the greatest things about overnight camps is that they offer kids a change from their usual school and home environments. A well-supervised coed overnight camp may be a welcome change for some kids, especially teenagers.

Coed camps also have an advantage for families with both a boy and a girl who want to go to camp. It's convenient to drop your son and daughter off at the same camp. They may even enjoy spending time together there. However, the convenience of a single drop-off site is minimal if the advantages of a single-sex camp are important to you. As an alternative to searching for a coed camp, find out whether the single-sex camps you like have a nearby "brother camp" or "sister camp." Many camps have this kind of formal affiliation with each other. Usually, brother and sister camps are of similar quality and have similar philosophies. They may even have the same change days and visiting days, to make it easy for parents. Most brother-sister camps are within an hour's drive of each other.

Coed camps, however, vary in how much they integrate the boys and the girls. At some coed camps, boys and girls may sleep and change in separate cabins, but do everything else together. At other coed camps, boys and girls are kept apart, but eat together in the same dining hall. Some camps promote themselves as single-sex camps, but they have a sister camp or a brother camp on the same property. It's important to find out how much boys and girls are integrated in these settings.

When making your choice of single-sex vs. coed, you should also consider the camp's program offerings. If you want a camp with a lot of sports, then a single-sex camp may be best because the competition will be more fair. If you prefer a camp with a strong academic or fine arts program, then a coed environment may be best. If the camp has a mixed program of athletics and academics or fine arts, find out whether boys and girls do the athletic activities together. Sometimes coed athletics are phenomenal; other times, they're unrealistic.

Finally, you should consider staff issues. More so than a single-sex staff, coed staff members are likely to have other business on their minds besides making sure that campers are having a fun time. Directors of coed camps often regret how the inevitable staff romances impair instruction and interfere with cabin leadership. Staff members at coed camps may also be distracted by campers who have crushes on them.

Of course, crushes are normal and romantic love is wonderful. It's just that romance can detract from the goals of any camp—coed or single-sex. Plus, kids deemed less romantically desirable will feel the same rejection at camp that they do at home among their coed classmates. Single-sex camps allow most kids to dismiss that issue for a while. About 50% of all overnight camps are single-sex.

4. What kind of organization do you want?

Overnight camps vary in size from fewer than 90 campers to more than 400, but all sizes and types have some kind of organizational structure. The two main components are *living* (how the living quarters are organized) and *activities* (how the activity periods are organized). Understanding your child's living and activity preferences will help you select the best camp.

Organization of Living Quarters

Most overnight camps organize campers' living quarters by age or school grade. This is the organization that makes kids most comfortable.

Grouping camper's living quarters by age or grade makes it easier for kids to change clothes in front of one another, for cabin leaders to select age-appropriate activities the whole cabin will enjoy, and for each group to have its own identity.

The typical organization of living quarters at a traditional overnight camp hasn't changed in more than a century. The entire camp is usually divided into three, four, or five units or *divisions,* according to the age or grade of the campers. Each division comprises several cabins. Each cabin contains between 6 and 20 campers and between 1 and 4 cabin leaders. Cabin leaders live and eat with the children and may also function as activity instructors. There are variations, but this is how most traditional overnight camps organize their living quarters.

The organization of living quarters at specialty overnight camps and special needs camps varies. Camps with their own outdoor property usually organize their living arrangements like a traditional camp, by age or grade. Camps that use college campuses usually have a less structured organization. There, it's more likely that younger kids will be living next door to, or even in the same room with, older kids. On college campuses, it's also less likely that an adult leader will be living in the same room with your child. This organization of living quarters results in less direct supervision and guidance. Such leadership from a distance will make it difficult for your child to benefit from the positive adult role models who work at the camp. Living quarters should be organized to provide outstanding supervision and leadership to all children, all the time.

Regardless of the exact organization of living quarters, remember that any adult who actually lives with campers is like a substitute parent. That person's job is to befriend your child, set an example for her, encourage her when she is challenged, praise her when she succeeds, support her when she fails, and comfort her when she is down. It's important that such an adult be extremely well trained in leadership, gifted at working with kids, tremendously enthusiastic, and consistently aware of appropriate limits and boundaries.

Organization of Activity Periods

Activity periods are organized differently at different camps. There's no single best way to organize activity periods at an overnight camp. It depends on the camp's philosophy, the staff's skills, the kind of kids who attend the camp, the climate, and the facilities that are available.

The organization of activity periods ranges from *maximum structure* to *almost complete freedom.* At every overnight camp, there are some scheduled activities that all campers must do, such as getting up in the morning and eating at a certain time. Most camps also offer a few choices of what to do and when to do it. However, the variation in structure is great.

At the *maximum structure* end of the spectrum, you will find camps that schedule all the activities for kids ahead of time. For example, if you're in Cabin 3, you'll play baseball from 9:30 to 11:00, go swimming from 11:20 to 12:00, then eat lunch from 12:15 to 1:00, and so on. There are advantages to such high structure. Kids get to:

- Try new activities they might not have chosen on their own
- Know what's coming up next
- Rely on staff to schedule full and interesting days for them
- Get better at activities they plan to repeat each day

There are also disadvantages to such high structure. Kids may:

- Be scheduled to do less enjoyable activities
- Not get to do their favorite activities as often as they wish
- Do everything with the same group of kids all day
- Miss the fun of choosing a personalized schedule
- Not have enough time to relax and just hang out

At the *almost complete freedom* end of the spectrum, you will find camps that offer endless choices. There may be several blocks of time each day when campers can choose among six or eight different activities. For example, from 9:30 to 11:50, campers may have the choice between basket weaving, horseback riding, sailing, volleyball, swimming lessons, snorkeling, and riflery. There are advantages to such freedom. Kids get to:

- Have fun choosing what they want to do, and when they want to do it
- Plan to do some of their favorite activities every day

- Be with different groups of kids and staff at different activities
- Build in enough time to relax and just hang out

There are also disadvantages to such freedom. Kids may:

- Never try anything new because no one makes them
- Feel lazy and not go to any activities (They might as well be sitting at home.)
- Get overwhelmed by the number of choices
- Fail to improve at any one thing because they're always trying something new

As you might guess, there are many camps that strike a balance between high structure and almost complete freedom. At these camps, staff schedule some activity periods ahead of time and kids choose the rest. Your child might do some activities with his cabin mates but other activities with kids from other cabins. This balance is a good concept, but it too has some disadvantages. For example, when lots of campers choose the same activity, and there isn't enough room or equipment for everyone, some kind of selection needs to happen. Raffles and lotteries are the most fair ways of selecting who gets to do the activity and who has to choose something else. The best camps keep track of who loses each raffle, to give those kids first priority the next time that activity is offered. The best camps also modify activities appropriately when just a few campers show up for a period.

Two final notes on activity period organization: First, not all campers get to do all activities. Second, some camps charge extra money to a camper's account for certain activities. For example, water-skiing might cost $5 extra per run, to defray the cost of gasoline for the boat; horseback riding might cost $100 extra per week, to pay for the horses' care. If your child likes the idea of freedom to choose activities at camp, make sure you know which activities he is eligible to do, and which have an additional fee. Restricted activities and those that cost extra should be noted in the camp's registration materials.

CHAPTER 6

Step 2: Gather Information

In preparing to write this chapter, we sent away for information from hundreds of camps throughout the country, printed out reams of camp web pages from the Internet, and bought camp reference books. Within a few weeks, we had built a precarious tower of brochures, information sheets, and videotapes. Each showed smiling children doing fun activities; each guaranteed a great time. We developed a renewed appreciation for the challenge of picking a camp. With nearly 6,300 overnight camps in the United States, the process of gathering information can be as long as you want it to be. By the time you sifted through 6,300 brochures and videos, your child would be sending his own children to camp.

To simplify the search process, use the following step-by-step checklist and search only for the type of camp in which you're interested. After reading Chapters 4 and 5, you should know what type of camp you're looking for, as well as the distance, location, length of stay, gender mix, and organization you prefer. If you have not yet decided some of these issues, that's OK, but your gathering of information will be less focused and may take considerably longer.

At the back of this book there is an extensive *Resources & references* section that lists camping organizations, Internet sites, sources for special needs programs, community organizations, books and much more.

As before, we've provided a checklist to track your progress. You can see by skimming it that the goal of this chapter is to make a list. Your list will have the names and addresses of a dozen or more specific camps that you and your child find appealing. At the end of the chapter, you'll use this list to request a packet of information from each camp. Then, in Chapter 7, we'll show you how to evaluate those packets and narrow your selection to a single camp.

Don't worry about doing everything on the list, or even doing it in order. We've written this chapter in the order that works best for most people, but a different order may work for you. As long as you are thorough in your search, you will have an excellent chance of finding a high-quality camp that matches your budget, your preferences, and your tough standards.

Before you start:

❑ Buy a pack of 3" x 5" index cards or a small spiral-bound notebook on which to write information about camps.

❑ Use the following template (or one like it) for keeping track of information on each camp. Write each camp on a separate card or notebook page.

Camp name: _____

Source of information: _____

Phone: _____ Fax: _____ Internet: _____

Mailing address: _____

_____

Notes: _____

_____

Checklist:

Step 1: Start at home.

❏ Find out what overnight camps your family members attended and recommend.

❏ Find out what overnight camps your friends, and your child's friends and classmates, attended and recommend.

Step 2: Branch into the community.

❏ Ask for recommendations and information at your place of worship, if you have one.

❏ Ask for recommendations and information at community organizations.

Step 3: Explore your region.

❏ Contact your regional American Camping Association office.

❏ Look in newspapers, especially the classifieds, for advertisements.

❏ Go to a camp fair. Talk to camp staff and collect literature there.

❏ Visit some local camps to get a flavor for what's out there.

❏ Consider employing a personal consultant or using a free referral source, such as the National Camp Association.

Step 4: Go national/international.

❏ Buy a camp reference book or use the library

❏ Read a few national newspapers and magazines.

❏ Search for information on the Internet.

Step 5: Send away for information.

❏ Gather your index cards or notebook. This is your goal: Make a list.

❏ Send away for an information packet from each camp on the list and store it all in one box or file.

Step 1: Start at home.

Your Family's Camp Experience

If grandparents, parents, relatives, or siblings have gone to overnight camp before, that's the best place to start gathering information. The

camps that older family members attended might still be around, although they may have changed in quality and substance. Find out what your relatives liked and disliked about the camps they attended. If they recommend a certain camp, fill out an index card or notebook page with the relevant contact information.

Beware of you own biases as a parent. Your favorite camp from a generation ago may not meet your child's needs and interests. As former campers and current staff members, we know how strong one's attachment to a particular camp can be. You may greatly desire your son or daughter to have the same camping experience you did. However, you still need do some research. The character of a camp can change with a new director or a shift in philosophy. Just because you enjoyed it 20 or 30 years ago doesn't guarantee your child will like it today.

Friends

A lot of people hear about a specific camp from a family friend. You know from our little autobiographies in Chapter 1 that we ended up at overnight camp because friends recommended it. Luckily for us, we ultimately loved our camp experiences. However, we had both gone to other day and overnight camps that we didn't like very much. Those, too, were recommended by friends. What's the lesson here? Just because you trust someone as a friend does not mean you should close this book and rush to that camp. Although your friend's choice could turn out to be a great one for your child too, every family has different interests, needs, and resources. You owe it to yourself and your child to gather information on other camps.

The advantage of getting information from a friend or family member is that it's first-hand. It's also a perfect opportunity for your child to ask other kids what they thought of overnight camp. They can think of questions and discuss things that might never occur to adults. After gathering opinions from parents and kids with camp experience, write the highlights of what they said on the index card or notebook page that you've started for that camp.

Just for kids

Questions to Ask Other Kids about Overnight Camp

1. How did you like camp?
2. What was the best thing about your camp?
3. What was the worst thing about your camp?
4. What were the other kids like?
5. What were the cabin leaders like?
6. How were the activities? Did you get good instruction?
7. Did you get to do what you wanted?
8. How was the food? Was there enough?
9. Were there any special events? What were they?
10. Would you go back again to the same camp? Why or why not?

Step 2: Branch into the community.

Places of Worship

There are two ways to gather information at your place of worship, if you attend one. The first is to find out whether the organization sponsors its own camp. If you're looking for a religious specialty camp, this is your best bet. Even if the organization doesn't sponsor its own camp, the clergy may have contacts with a related religious organization that does run a camp. The second way is to talk to other families. Presumably, these families share similar values, so they may have had experience with an overnight camp that would also please your family.

Community Organizations

There are many community organizations that either sponsor or provide information on overnight camps. Examples include the Rotary Club, the Lions Club, the Kiwanis Club, the YMCA, the YWCA, Young Judaea, the YMHA (Young Men's Hebrew Association), Boy Scouts of America, Girl Scouts USA, the United Way, 4-H, Camp Fire Boys and Girls, and your local school system. If you or someone you know belongs to one of these organizations, ask them for a recommendation. Otherwise, you can call, write, or stop by the chapter office and get whatever information they have on local camps. If any of their recommendations match your preferences for type, location, length of stay, gender mix, and structure, fill out an index card or a notebook page so that you can send for a packet of information later on.

If you're looking for a special needs camp, you should ask for recommendations from the health care professionals who know your child. If your child is treated at a hospital, ask the staff for camp recommendations. (Hospital staff often volunteer at special needs camps.) You should also contact the national association that corresponds to your child's special needs. For example, the American Burn Association can provide a listing of all the burn camps across the country. Because they are sponsored by national and regional organizations, many of these special needs camps cost very little. Some are even free. It pays to call around.

Step 3: Explore your region.

Beyond your circle of family, friends, and community organizations, there are many regional sources of information. Here are some ways to gather information on camps in your state and neighboring states.

Regional Offices of the American Camping Association

Call or write to your regional office of the American Camping Association (ACA). (Contacts are in the back of this book.) Ask them to send you a listing of overnight camps in your area. You may also be able to request listings of a certain type of camp, such as a specialty music camps or environmental education camps. Your regional ACA office is an excellent source of information about camps near you. However, their listings may not include some camps that are not accredited by the ACA. Therefore, you should also gather information from other regional sources.

What is the ACA?

The American Camping Association, headquartered in Martinsville, Indiana, describes itself as "a community of camp professionals dedicated to enriching the lives of children and adults through the camp experience. Founded in 1910, ACA is the only nationally recognized body which accredits all types of camps throughout the United States." (Source: *Guide to ACA-Accredited Camps*)

Camp directors make up the Association's primary membership. Each year, the ACA sponsors national and regional conferences for camp professionals to share ideas, network, and enhance their skills. Although the ACA is a for-profit organization, it raises a lot of money for camper scholarships and public education. The ACA is nonsectarian, but many religiously-affiliated camps are ACA members. All member camps pay yearly dues to the association.

Local Newspapers

Local and regional newspapers can be a good source of information on overnight camps. Some local papers print camp advertisements in the classified section; other papers actually publish listings of camps in your area or state. These ads and listings are most prevalent in the winter and spring, when camps are trying to fill their sessions, but we see them all year round in some papers.

Camp Fairs

Secondary schools, colleges, universities, scouting groups, YMCAs, and various community organizations sometimes sponsor camp fairs. These fairs are usually held in a school cafeteria, gymnasium, or community center. Generally, each camp will have a representative at the fair who sits at a booth or table, hands out literature on the camp, and answers questions from parents and children. Feel free to ask any questions you have about the camp, including the type, location, length of stay options, gender mix, and activities.

We like camp fairs for two reasons: You get to talk to a person from the camp, and you get to compare many camps simultaneously. Even if your child is not interested in going to overnight camp this year, it's a good idea to go to a camp fair to learn what kinds of camps are around. Pick up literature and ask questions. Then, next year, if your child shows interest in camp, send for new, updated brochures. To find out about camp fairs, look in your local newspaper (especially the classified section), call the school district, ask around at community organizations when you visit them, or call your regional ACA office.

Visit Local Camps

If you have time, visiting a local camp can teach you a lot. Visits are a great way to gather information. Just be sure to call ahead. If the camp is

in session, random visits from interested families can be disruptive. If the camp is not in session, remember that it's not going to look as good as when it is in session. The off-season is when camps do their maintenance, so there's likely to be some construction going on, and most equipment will be put away. Still, a visit will give you some idea about the beauty of the property, the facilities, and the overall structure of the camp.

Referral Sources

You can gather regional information, and maybe save some time, by talking to a referral source. There are two kinds: freelance consultants and organized services. Freelance consultants—who may or may not charge a fee—are people who offer to find you a matching camp by interviewing you and then making a recommendation. Some consultants are excellent; others are less skilled. None of them has any kind of official certification in selecting camps, and their level of experience varies. Be sure to ask a lot of questions. For example:

- What is your personal camping experience?
- How long have you been in the consulting business?
- Have you visited many camps, including the ones you

recommend? Or, are you basing your recommendations only on what you've heard about different camps?

- Can you provide names of other satisfied clients? If not, why not?
- Do you work only with some camps and not others? If so, why? What kinds of special agreements do you have with camps?
- Do you work on commission? If you're taking a percentage of the camp tuition, are you only recommending expensive camps?
- If I have to pay you, is my satisfaction guaranteed? If my child and I don't like the camp, must I still pay?

Organized referral services are an alternative to freelance consultants. Some organizations, such as the American Camping Association's regional offices or the National Camp Association, will make free referrals. Camps pay membership fees to belong to either organization, so neither is unbiased. However, the ACA and NCA differ in the sources of information they provide. ACA referrals come from a database of thousands of member camps, accredited with rigorous inspection standards. By comparison, the NCA draws from a significantly smaller database of both accredited and non-accredited camps that have been visited by NCA staff and evaluated by some parents and campers. To initiate an NCA or ACA referral, check the *Resources & references* section.

Finally, you can call any camp you're interested in and ask for a short list of veteran parents in your area with whom you can talk. Many camps will provide you with the names and numbers of families who are happy to talk about their experience with that particular overnight camp. Many referral families will have had experiences with other camps, too, and can tell you why they prefer one camp over another.

Step 4: Go national/international.

To learn more about overnight camps, you'll want to extend your search across the country. Those of you who are fairly certain that you want to go to camp close to home should skim this next section. Some of the information sources we discuss are helpful for local and regional searches as well.

Reference Books

There are some large reference books that can help you find interesting camps across the country, and even across the world, that fit your selection criteria. These references vary in price from under $10 to over $30. As economical alternatives to purchasing such books, check your local library or share the cost with another family who is also gathering camp information.

The most thorough printed reference for camps is the American Camping Association's *Guide to ACA-Accredited Camps*. Updated annually, this book lists over 2,200 day and overnight camps by region. A nice feature of the ACA *Guide* is that, in addition to the standard alphabetical index of accredited camps, the book has two special sections: one that lists camps with specific philosophies, and one that lists camps for children with special needs.

For each camp listed in the ACA *Guide*, you will find contact information, a short description of the camp's philosophy and activities, session information, enrollment size, age range of the campers, and cost. The cost information is a bit vague. Tuition is expressed as a range, such as $301-$500 per week, so you'll have to contact the camp to get exact prices. This is an excellent reference book, but remember that some quality camps are not members of the ACA, and non-member camps are not listed. The ACA *Guide* costs about $20.

Another helpful reference is *Frost's Summer Camp Guide*. Although it only profiles about 650 day and overnight camps, the price is economical, usually under $10. The information presented in *Frost's* is similar to that provided in the ACA *Guide*, but the cost information is more specific, and the camps listed include both accredited and non-accredited camps. Like the ACA *Guide*, *Frost's* has sections on special programs and camps for children with special needs, as well as an alphabetical camp index.

A unique feature of *Frost's* is that it offers a tuition discount of 25% for some of the camps listed. The way this works is that camps in *Frost's* pay for advertising space. In return for this promotion, some camps offer a limited number of discounted registrations. If you're interested in one of the camps that offers this deal, you could save money. However, the discounted tuition spots go quickly, so contact the Frost company as soon as you've identified your first choice.

The third major reference book is *Peterson's Summer Opportunities for Kids & Teenagers*. This telephone-book-size reference covers over 1,800 summer programs, including overnight camps, teen tours, academic programs, wilderness adventures, and specialty sports and fine arts workshops. There are also many international programs listed. The breadth of this reference makes it a good resource for parents and kids who want to expand their search for information beyond overnight camps.

Two unique features of *Peterson's* are its careful organization and its detail. There's a 40-page quick-reference chart that gives key facts about the 1,800 different programs, such as gender mix, age range, and program activity basics. The chart will help you and your child narrow your search for the right camp or program. At the back of the book is a standard alphabetical index, plus a great section that has all the programs organized into one of eight categories: academic options, arts, special-interest activities, sports, travel components, wilderness/outdoors activities, accommodations for children with special needs, and religious affiliations.

The bulk of the book is a detailed, 1,100-page descriptive section, including 300 in-depth descriptions of various programs, some of which are overnight camps. The in-depth descriptions include details on location, background and philosophy, program offerings, enrollment, daily schedule, facilities, staff, costs, financial aid, transportation, application timetable, and contact information. *Peterson's* costs about $30.

National Newspapers

National papers, such as the *New York Times* and the *Los Angeles Times*, often publish overnight summer camp supplements in the late winter and early spring. You can also find advertisements for different camps in the Sunday magazine sections of these and other national papers. National newspapers are available in large libraries and bookstores. Unfortunately, it's hard to know exactly when the papers will publish a section on overnight camp. Remember, too, that many camps do not advertise much, or at all. Don't consider the listing in any newspaper comprehensive or representative. A full-page advertisement may look spiffy, but it could mean that the camp is struggling for business. If this is the case, you have to wonder why.

The Internet

Camps have discovered that the Internet is a great way to advertise. Thousands of camps now have their own web pages. A few more just got added in the time it took us to write this sentence. If you have Internet access, through your local library, school, or home computer, this can be a great way to search for camps. Like any search on the Internet, you will have to sift through much fluff before finding substance. With a bit of perseverance, you could find just what you're looking for.

Camp web sites offer unique features: colorful, interactive pictures and up-to-date information. Your child might even be able to take virtual tours of certain camps. However, keep in mind that advertising is advertising, and just because a camp is on-line does not mean that it's any better or worse than one that is not. If a camp in which you are interested does not have a web site, don't assume it is behind the times. It may not need any additional advertising, or it may be taking a philosophic stance against electronic media.

There are two basic methods we recommend you use to search the Internet for camp web sites. The first is to search for the keywords "camp" or "summer camp" using your favorite commercial search engine. The second is to go to an organization's web site and use its own micro search engine. Often this second method will be faster and more organized, but you never know what helpful information you'll find if you search on your own. Remember to bookmark or print out the web sites you like so you can refer back to the information later.

Step 5: Send away for information.

This last step is simple. You've gathered information from a variety of sources and written down the names and addresses of dozens of camps. You've achieved the goal of this chapter by making a list of your favorites. Now it's time to send a letter or postcard to each of those camps to request an information packet. In your correspondence, we suggest that you ask for "information for parents and kids on the upcoming camp season, including all registration materials." By requesting registration materials now, you're saving yourself time later.

How many camps should you write to? There's really no minimum or maximum. Even if you have your heart set on one particular camp, it's still a good idea to write away for information from your second, third, fourth, and fifth choices. Your first-choice camp may be full this year. Plus, when you have information from several camps, you can compare the strengths and weaknesses of each. It's not time to narrow your selection just yet. Write to every camp that looks like a possibility. Families who don't have a clear first-choice camp should write to at least a dozen different camps. It hardly costs you anything to request the material, and the more data you have, the more informed your choice will be.

CHAPTER 7

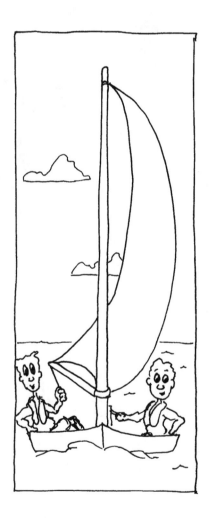

Step 3: Choose the best camp for you

In this chapter, you'll complete the selection process by learning how to evaluate all those information packets you've received. Read this chapter first to become a savvy consumer, then comb through your camp materials with a critical eye.

There are five basic elements to evaluate in any camp: Features, Character, Quality, Service, and Cost. Each element is composed of several key questions, and each question has many associated issues. No family needs to examine every issue.

The checklist below will guide you and your child through this final stage in the selection process. As usual, you don't have to complete it in order. However, you should review the entire checklist to ensure that the camp you choose meets your requirements.

Checklist

Step 0: Send away for information

❏ If you don't have a pile of camp information packets, then you must have skipped Chapter 6. Go back and gather the information you need before you start this chapter.

Step 1: Evaluate the camp's features.

❑ Does your child like the variety and type of activities? Do some activities cost extra?

❑ Are the facilities and equipment in good shape? Are they what your child wants? Can campers bring their own equipment?

❑ Is the dining cafeteria-style, family-style, or something else? Are the foods on the menu appetizing? Do they meet your child's dietary needs?

❑ Is the variety of natural landscapes and man-made environments pleasing? Is the atmosphere of the camp commercial or natural?

❑ Does your child like the way the camp structures the daily schedule, program choices, and grouping of campers? Are his favorite activities available often?

Step 2: Evaluate the camp's character.

❑ What kind of reputation and background does the camp have? Have there been significant staff, leadership, or facility changes lately? Why?

❑ What experience and qualifications does the director have? Is she easy to relate to? Does she have a background in teaching or a child-related profession?

❑ Are the camp's traditions, mix of other children, and manners an asset?

❑ Are the camp's mission, values, and discipline style appealing? How do cabin leaders provide support when campers need it? Do these philosophies match your own?

Step 3: Evaluate the camp's quality.

❑ Is the camp accredited by the American Camping Association? (Many good camps are not, but this is one factor to consider.)

❑ How qualified are the instructors? Are instructors of high-risk programs certified?

❑ Are most staff certified in first aid and CPR?

❑ What is the camp's safety record?

❑ Are the staff, especially the cabin leaders, experienced and well-trained? Were they recruited from outside the camp, or were they once campers at that camp? Are they promoted based on how well they work with children? What is the average tenure of cabin leaders?

❑ Do the international cabin leaders and instructors speak fluent English?

❑ What is the real camper-to-leader ratio? How much time do cabin leaders actually spend with their campers each day?

❑ Is the camp's health center clean and well-equipped? Is the medical staff qualified? Is there a hospital and/or a doctor affiliated with the camp, in case of emergencies?

Step 4: Evaluate the camp's service.

❑ Are you comfortable with the ways you can contact camp in an emergency? Is it clear who is in charge at the camp?

❑ Are you comfortable with the ways the camp permits parents and children to stay in contact, by phone, visits, letters, faxes, or e-mail?

❑ Are kids immersed in the camp environment, or is their stay disrupted by the outside world of television, shopping malls, and random visitors?

Step 5: Evaluate the camp's cost.

❑ Can you afford the cost of the camp? Is it a good value?

❑ Are the tuition, fees, and spending money allocations reasonable? Do they cover everything you want?

❑ If the cost of the camps you like seems too high, have you researched scholarships? Even if you don't need a scholarship, what ways can your child help earn money for camp?

Step 6: Conduct personal interviews and inspections.

❏ Narrow your list down to five or six camps using Steps 1-5 above.

❏ Contact the directors of those five or six camps and ask them any unanswered questions that you have.

❏ Contact personal references (parents and children who know the camp) and ask them about their experiences.

❏ If possible, schedule a time with the camp director when you can visit the camp and inspect its environment, atmosphere, facilities, and equipment yourself.

Buyer beware

A word of caution before you start: Promotional materials that camps publish, such as colorful brochures and video tapes, are advertisements.

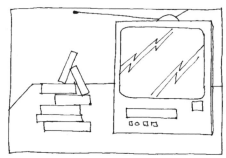

The camp is trying to sell itself to you by emphasizing its best parts. Remember, though, that you need to know about all parts of a camp before you can make a wise choice. Choosing a camp based on a few attractive pictures or a few smiling faces is like buying a car because it's painted a pretty color. If the promotional material you receive from a camp doesn't answer the questions relevant to you, you'll need to dig deeper.

Step 1: Evaluate the camp's features.

When evaluating a camp, you should ask: What does the camp feature? What kinds of activities, facilities, environment, and structure does the camp provide? Here are the specifics:

What activities does the camp offer?

- **Variety.** Traditional camps offer a wide variety of activities. Are the activities your child likes on the list? Are there some activities he's never tried before?

- **Specialty.** Specialty camps have one or two primary activities. However, even these camps should offer some variety. For example, a basketball camp might also include swimming in its program so that campers don't get bored or burned out. Are there some activities your child likes besides the camp's specialty?

- **Special needs.** Special needs camps adapt activities to the campers' abilities However, special needs camps are all different, even if they work with the same type of children. Will your child be supported, entertained, and challenged?

- **Fees.** Certain fun and popular activities cost extra at some camps. For example, tennis may be included in the camp tuition, but activities such as water-skiing, go-carts, ham radio, rocketry, dirt bikes, trips, and horseback riding may cost an additional fee. Do the activities your child plans to do cost extra? Do they fit your budget?

What are the camp's facilities and equipment like?

- **Facilities.** Living, bathing, and activity facilities should be neat, clean, and in good condition. Looking at the camp's brochure, web site, video, or CD-ROM may tell you something about the facilities, but talking to someone who has been to the camp will teach you more. Of course, there's no substitute for actually visiting the camp. If you can schedule a visit to the camp, check to see whether the facilities are well-maintained and adequate for the activities that take place there.

- **Equipment.** Campers with advanced skills have certain facility and equipment preferences. Serious soccer players prefer regulation-size goals, not small nets. Serious marksmen prefer match rifles, not BB guns. Serious swimmers prefer swimming areas with turning boards and lane lines, not bare dock pilings. If your child has some advanced skills, find out whether the camp has the equipment she prefers. Don't forget that kids can often bring their own equipment, such as a baseball glove or a tennis racket. Some kids prefer personal gear over the camp's equipment.

- **Dining Hall.** The dining hall is one facility that all kids want to know about. As you learned in Chapter 4, there are two basic types: cafeteria style and family style. Either style can be structured, where campers sit with their cabin mates, or open, where kids pick their own seats. Both styles usually offer some food choices, but no camp serves everybody's favorite food all the time.

If your child is a picky eater, or if he has special dietary restrictions, learn whether the camp offers the sorts of food he can eat. If you have concerns, we recommend that you ask the camp to send you a week-long sample menu. Do the choices on the menu look good, or is the same food served at every meal? Are there daily salad bar or sandwich options for kids who don't like the main course?

What is the camp's environment like?

- **Type of Environment.** As we mentioned earlier, overnight camps offer various environments. The camp you choose may be in the mountains, on a lake, or on a school campus. Most camps are proud of their combination of natural and man-made environments. Indeed, this variety may be the most important aspect of any camp environment. Does the camp's environment suit your child?

- **Atmosphere.** Don't be too impressed with acreage. A camp may boast 300 or 3000 acres of property but have crummy facilities. It's really the combination of space, environment, facilities, and staff that creates the camp's atmosphere. Some camps have a commercial, artificial, country club atmosphere. Other camps have a more natural wilderness atmosphere. Has the camp used its land thoughtfully?

What is the structure of the camp?

- **Daily Schedule.** Every camp has a daily schedule. There are wake-up times, meal times, activity times, and maybe chore times and free times. These times help structure your child's life at camp, but this structure may be quite different from his schedule at home. For example, he may sleep until noon on vacation days, but he'll have to get up between 7:00 a.m. and 8:00 a.m. at camp. Does your child think the daily camp schedule is reasonable and enjoyable?

- **Program Choices.** As we discussed in Chapter 5, some camps offer kids the freedom to make activity choices. Other camps require kids to participate in certain activities at certain times. Many camps are structured to offer a combination of choices and requirements. This helps kids try new things they might have otherwise ignored. Will your child get to choose the activities he does each day? Or, is he happy to have someone else schedule most of his day?

- **Activity Availability.** In camps where kids get to choose their activities, find out how often certain activities are available. For example, if your child plans to choose archery every day then it's important to know whether archery is actually offered every day. A few camps use exotic activities, like rocketry, ham radio, or dirt bikes to attract business, but it may turn out those activities are not offered more than once a week. Is your child content with how often her favorite activities are offered?

- **Grouping of Campers.** Remember, a big part of a camp's structure is how the kids are grouped. Most frequently, campers are grouped by age or school grade into cabins or divisions. They feel most comfortable that way. If your child is the only 9-year-old in a cabin of 14-year-olds, she may feel awkward. Is your child comfortable with the way campers are grouped? Are there enough other campers her age?

  Of course, some contact with substantially older and younger kids can be fun and helpful. We especially like camps that have a "big brothers" or "big sisters" program, where older, veteran campers are paired with younger, less experienced campers. These programs are great ways for younger campers to feel welcomed, and for older campers to develop leadership skills.

Step 2: Evaluate the camp's character.

When evaluating a camp, you should ask: What is the background, tradition, and philosophy of the camp? Here are the specifics:

What is the camp's background?

- **Reputation.** A few camps in the country have been around since the turn of the century. Others began a few years ago.

Older camps are not necessarily better, but they are easier to evaluate because they have a long performance record. When did the camp start, and how has its reputation evolved over the years?

- **Recent changes.** Specialty camps and special needs camps often change a lot from year to year. Has the director, the staff, the sports star, the location, or the sponsor of the camp changed recently? Have there been major facility changes? Why have those changes taken place, and how will they affect the camp?

- **The Director.** The background of the director is important because he or she is the guiding force for the entire camp. Men and women with a prior background in camping, teaching, coaching, or child care tend to be more skilled and compassionate camp directors than those with a background in an unrelated field.

  Some camp directors have completed the ACA's Camp Director's Institute or its Basic Camp Director's Course; others simply have a wealth of field experience. Does the camp director have a strong background, a good reputation, and a lot of experience working with kids?

- **Publicity.** Publicity, for either good or bad reasons, can shape

the reputation of a camp. Don't believe everything you read in the papers or see on television. Some famous camps are just a name. Some great camps may have been rocked by a recent scandal or accident, generating a temporary bad reputation. Look beyond any media publicity to see what sort of camp is truly behind the opinion of one lone reporter.

What are the camp's traditions?

- **Traditions.** Every camp has traditions. Thoughtful traditions, such as vespers services, create a positive atmosphere and make campers feel part of something important. If there are religious or spiritual traditions, be sure you and your child are comfortable with them. (You may wish to turn back to the discussion of religious and spiritual traditions in Chapter 5.) If there are Native American traditions, find out whether these are authentic and respectful.

- **Clientele.** An unofficial tradition that most camps have is a certain ethnic or socioeconomic clientele. Some camps have mostly rich, European-American children; other camps have mostly middle-income children of minority ethnicity. Still other camps have a diverse mix of kids from different backgrounds and ethnicities. Fortunately, more and more camps offer scholarships to children from low-income families.

  There is no single cultural, economic, or ethnic formula that is best. Certain mixes of kids suit certain camps, and different families have different preferences. Does the camp you and your child are considering have a tradition of attracting the mix of kids you seek?

- **Manners.** All camps have a traditional level of manners. Some camps tolerate swearing; other camps forbid all profanity. Some camps observe table manners and offer a blessing before each meal. At other camps, mealtime is a giant food-fight, and cabin leaders don't even sit with their campers. Do the manners at the camp meet your standards?

What are the camp's philosophies?

A camp's philosophies are difficult to glean from its own promotional materials. Your best sources of information are the camp director, parents of kids who have attended the camp, and veteran campers.

- **Mission.** One good way to learn about the camp's philosophy is to read its mission statement. As we discussed in Chapter 2, mission statements all sound good, but it's hard to know whether a camp's mission is ever accomplished. Ask your sources questions such as, "Do you feel the mission statement or motto was a mere slogan or a way of life?" and "How exactly is the camp's mission statement or motto put into practice?"

- **Values.** The camp's values rub off on its campers. What does each camp value? Some camps value competition over participation. There may be lots of team activities, but less skilled children rarely get to play. Other camps value skill development over fun. Each child improves her skill in certain areas, but she may not have a chance to do other fun activities. Some camps emphasize new games, which have no winners or losers. Other camps think winning and losing are valuable life lessons that shape a child's self-esteem.

Which values are best is a personal and sometimes controversial topic. It's up to you and your child to decide that. Ask your sources questions such as, "How competitive is the camp?" "Do kids have to fit a certain stereotype to be accepted?" "What do cabin leaders do to make the kids feel part of the group?" "How, if at all, do kids change during their camp stay?"

- **Discipline.** The camp's discipline philosophy shapes campers' behavior. At one end of the spectrum are camps run in a strict, military fashion; at the other end are camps so permissive that campers' behavior spins out of control. Most camps are somewhere between these two extremes.

  Children feel safest when adult caregivers set clear limits and demonstrate examples of good behavior. High quality camps have experienced staff whose behavior sets a good example for the campers to follow. High quality camps also have staff who know how to handle behavioral problems in a responsible and even-tempered manner. Ask your sources questions such as, "How do the cabin leaders provide fair, effective discipline?" and "What do the cabin leaders do to help all campers feel comfortable and secure?"

- **Social Support.** The camp staff should know how to handle homesickness and other, normal emotional struggles that kids may encounter at camp. At a camp for children with special behavioral or emotional needs, you should expect even more expertise and professional training. Ask your sources questions such as, "How is the staff trained to support my child and meet his needs away from home?" and "What do the cabin leaders and instructors know about dealing with my child's special needs?"

Step 3: Evaluate the camp's quality.

When evaluating a camp, you should ask: What accreditation, certification, and training do the camp and its staff possess? These things don't guarantee high quality, but they set minimum requirements for health, safety, and skill. Here are the specifics:

Is the camp accredited?

- **Accreditation.** According to the American Camping Association, an ACA-accredited camp is one that has "met or

Points to Remember about Accreditation

As a smart shopper for camps, you must remember six things about accreditation.

1. Accreditation tells you a lot, but not everything, about the camp's quality. The ACA is an outstanding organization with very high inspection standards. However, some non-accredited camps set their own excellent standards.

2. No parent could ever inspect everything that trained inspectors do, so the ACA accreditation seal in the camp's brochure saves you a lot of time. If the camp is not ACA-accredited, you'll have to rely exclusively on its record and reputation. If you have extra time, you can also talk with the camp's director about his or her own standards for health, safety, staff training, and program quality.

3. If the camp passed its ACA inspection, then you can be certain it met or exceeded rigorous health, safety, staff-training, and program standards on the day it was inspected. Later that summer, or maybe two summers down the road, the camp could look quite different. The director may have changed, all the former staff may be gone, and the equipment could have taken a beating. ACA inspections happen once every three years. You want a camp that upholds its own high standards all the time.

4. No form of accreditation can prevent accidents. Things can and do go wrong at camps (and homes and schools) every year. Despite high standards, people make mistakes and equipment sometimes fails. Natural disasters occasionally occur. Kids get hurt from time to time.

5. ACA accreditation does not guarantee that your child will like the camp. Nothing can do that.

6. Camp = People. Camp is mostly about the people, not the facilities. No kind of accreditation will guarantee that the staff of the camp is skilled with children. As a close camp friend involved in leadership development once remarked, "Gifted cabin leaders could take a bunch of kids, put them in an empty parking lot, and turn it into a great camp."

exceeded the highest nationally recognized standards for health, safety, staff-training, and program quality." About 25% of the camps in the U.S. have earned ACA accreditation. Some 6% of camps who try for accreditation don't pass inspection; other camps are not interested in accreditation. Are the camps you're considering accredited, either by the ACA or by some other organization?

What certifications do instructors and cabin leaders have?

- **Instructor Certification.** Head instructors should be qualified to teach their program areas. For risky or technical programs, official certifications are a must. For example, the mini-golf instructor should have experience, but she doesn't need a certification in mini-golf, because it's not a risky or technical program. However, swimming instructors and lifeguards should be both experienced and certified because activities in the water involve risk. Do the camps you're considering have experienced and certified people in key programs?

- **First Aid/CPR Certification.** Both cabin leaders and instructors should be certified in basic first aid and CPR (cardiopulmonary resuscitation). Accidents do happen at camp and children may get hurt, despite the best efforts of an experienced staff. Has the camp trained its staff in first aid and CPR before the campers' arrival?

- **Qualifications and Safety Record.** ACA accreditation is a quick way to verify that a camp staff has the necessary qualifications. If the camp is not accredited, you yourself need to check the camp's safety record and staff qualifications. If the camp has a shaky reputation, a poor safety record, or an untrained staff, look elsewhere.

How skilled are the cabin leaders?

- **Experience.** The best cabin leaders are those with overnight camp experience. Their age is less important than how long they've been working with children. Most important, how long have the cabin leaders been working at that particular camp? At the highest quality camps, the cabin leaders return for many seasons in a row. What percentage of the staff is returning from last year? Anything above 50% suggests a particularly strong camp; above 75% staff return is extraordinary.

- **Training.** Before the campers arrive, all cabin leaders should receive in-service training in important areas, such as safety, leadership, discipline, program activities, and managing emotional and behavioral problems. What sort of training does the camp give its cabin leaders? Do they spend the pre-camp training week doing only hard labor to set up camp, or do they work to develop their skills with children?

- **Hiring and Promotion.** The manner in which cabin leaders are hired and promoted will tell you something about the camp's quality. Some camps advertise and recruit on college campuses, the Internet, and various places where young adults gather. Other camps have an internal promotion system whereby mature campers with leadership potential are invited to return as leaders-in-training. Both methods can yield high-quality cabin leaders. However, camp directors who use an internal promotion system really know the people they are hiring. At such camps, there tend to be fewer wild-card leaders who turn out to be poorly suited for the job. Where does the camp get its cabin leaders and instructors? What sort of interview and evaluation did they complete? How many were promoted from last year?

- **International Staff.** International staff add flair and diversity to any camp. At foreign language camps, they make especially wonderful contributions. At all other camps, it's critical that cabin leaders from other countries speak English (or whatever the primary language of the campers happens to be).

    Some camps boast about the international diversity of their staff. However, we've had kids tell us that, at their previous camp, their cabin leader didn't speak more than a few words of English. Not only is that annoying, there's also no way that a cabin leader can do her best if she doesn't speak the language of her campers. Does the camp hire international cabin leaders? (More than 50% do.) Are they fluent in your child's native language? If not, you probably want to choose a different camp.

What is the camper-to-leader ratio.

- **Camper-to-Leader Ration.** Many camps advertise their camper-to-leader ratio. The ratio is important, because the heart of the camping experience is the interaction between a cabin leader and his campers. If he is responsible for 20 children, each camper will spend only a few minutes a day with him. However, if the same cabin leader is responsible for only 9 children, then each child gets more attention.

  A problem lies in the way some camps calculate their camper-to-leader ratio. It's not valid to include the medical staff, maintenance staff, kitchen staff, and laundry staff in the calculation of this ratio. Such camps may say that they have a 5:1 camper-to-leader ratio, but each cabin actually has 14 campers and one leader. To find out the true ratio, learn how many children and how many leaders are in each cabin each day. A ratio between 4:1 and 10:1 is acceptable, with 6:1 being the national average. Also, check the daily camp schedule to see how much time cabin leaders actually spend with their campers. Will your child receive enough individual attention?

What is the quality of the camp's health center?

- **Health Center.** With luck, your child won't have to visit the camp's health center or infirmary more than once (on opening day). Still, you should see the health center and meet one of the staff, especially if your child has some specific medical concerns. The staff should be licensed to provide medical care to children, and the health center itself should be neat, clean, and well-stocked.

  Ask whether the medical staff lives at the camp or just comes in during their shifts. Our bias is that staff who live on-site have a better understanding of camp life and of the campers, which enables them to provide better care. If the camp has its own registered nurse (RN) or doctor (MD), does she live on-site, or is she just on-call? The farther a camp is from a hospital, the more important it becomes to have highly skilled medical staff who live at the camp.

Step 4: Evaluate the camp's service.

When evaluating a camp's service, you should ask: During camp, what kind of contact will there be between me, my child, the camp staff, and the outside world? Here are the specifics:

What sort of emergency contact do parents have with the camp?

- **Emergency Contact.** In an emergency, parents may need to contact the camp, or the camp may need to contact parents. Most camps have phones, but camps in remote locations may rely on two-way radios or cellular phones. Are you comfortable with the camp's link to the outside world? Will the camp contact you if your child is seriously injured or ill?

- **Person in Charge.** It's important to know who's in charge at the camp. Every camp has one or two directors. We mentioned above how important it is to know the camp director's background and experience. You must also know this person's name. You don't want to waste your time talking to a lower ranking staff person who doesn't have the authority or knowledge to assist you in an emergency.

What sort of regular contact do parents have with their children?

- **Phone.** All families ought to know their camp's phone policy. Some camps strictly forbid campers to use the phone, except in dire emergencies. These camps know that phone contact between parents and kids takes time away from activities and can amplify homesick feelings, at least temporarily. Other camps allow phone contact during certain hours of the day, or after campers have been at camp a certain number of days. These camps believe that phone conversations between parents and kids are sometimes encouraging. Not surprisingly, the "best" camp phone policy is an unsettled topic in the camping world.

   There are pros and cons to both policies, and we'll talk more about this issue, as well as visitation and letters, in Chapter 13. However, we'll say now that frequent phone contact defeats the "Nurture Independence" goal of overnight camping (see Chapter

2). Given your camping goals, are you and your child comfortable with the phone policy?

- **Visitation.** Parents and kids also want to know about the camp's visitation policy. Many camps have visiting days or a parents' weekend. Other camps allow open visitation, but only after a certain portion of the camp session has elapsed. Are you and your child comfortable with the camp's visitation policy?

- **Letters/Faxes/E-mail.** The traditional form of contact between parents and children at camp is letter writing. In addition, some camps make fax machines and e-mail available to campers. What kinds of written correspondence are possible at the camp?

What sort of regular contact do children have with the outside world?

- **On-Campus.** It's good for kids to stay immersed in the camp environment. The experience promotes a strong community without the distraction of television or the disruption of visitors who don't understand the spirit of the camp. Although urban or college-based camps tend to have more random people walking around, traditional camps also get outside visitors. What sort of non-camp people, if any, will your child meet during his stay? Is TV allowed?

- **Off-Campus.** We think it's unnecessary for cabin leaders to bring campers to the mall or to a nearby town to go shopping, buy candy, or attend a movie. These sorts of out-of-camp trips introduce a commercialism that ruins the camping atmosphere. By contrast, out-of-camp trips to hike a mountain or play sports against another camp's team are wonderful because they're in the spirit of overnight camping. What sort of out-of-camp trips do campers take?

Step 5: Evaluate the camp's cost.

When evaluating a camp, you should ask: What is the total cost, how can I pay for camp, and will I get my money's worth? Here are the specifics:

Why does it cost so much?

- **Profit.** One of the things that determines the price of a camp is whether it is non-profit or for-profit. Non-profit camps may be independent, religiously affiliated, or supported by an agency, such as the YMCA or Scouts. About 75% of all overnight camps are non-profit.

  For-profit camps are privately owned and independently run businesses. For-profit camps are generally more expensive, but that does not mean they are better.

  Overnight camp can be a big expense. Of course, most parents and kids agree that it's worth the investment. Learn about the camp's features, character, service, and quality before you decide the price tag is too high.

- **Expensive Camps.** Expensive camps charge big bucks to pay for specialized equipment, extravagant facilities, professional instructors, or luxurious out-of-camp trips. We know one camp that takes children to the nearest big city once a week to see major league baseball games. It's extravagant, but the campers love it. So, if you have the money for such a camp, and if you think your child would enjoy the program of activities, then consider enrolling. However, because price doesn't equal quality, check out some less expensive camps as well.

- **Average-Cost Camps.** It's hard to say what the average cost of overnight camp is. In 1999, the average camp cost between $250 and $800 a week if it was operated by a non-profit organization, youth group, or public agency. Privately-run camps and specialty camps cost between $350 and $1200 or more per week.

  This is a lot of money for most families, especially those considering multi-week stays for more than one child. The money goes to pay for some things you don't see, such as insurance, utility bills, and property tax. It also goes for things you do see, such as food, equipment, and staff. Remember, price does not equal quality, so it pays to shop around.

- **Free Camps.** Most free camps are sponsored by agencies, and they usually serve underprivileged children or children with special needs. Many are excellent. Do any organizations near you sponsor free or nearly free camps?

What are the tuition and fees, and what do they cover?
- **Tuition and Fees.** The cost of camp is usually broken down into two parts: tuition and fees. Tuition covers room, board, most activities, and most services, such as laundry. Fees cover things like the camp yearbook, some out-of-camp trips, certain activities, and special treats, such as a birthday cake if your child's birthday is during camp. What do tuition and fees cover at the camps you're considering?

- **Spending Money.** Spending money is sometimes treated as a separate fee. To discourage kids from carrying cash, the office may set up an account for each camper. The campers then draw credit from their accounts to purchase supplies or pay for special activities. If the camp does have spending money accounts, deposit the recommended amount. Camps know what an average camper spends. Any remaining balance will be refunded to you on closing day.

What if we can't afford the camp we like best?
- **Financial Options.** You have several options if you can't afford the camp you like best. First, more than 55% of all camps offer full or partial scholarships to families who cannot afford the full tuition and fees. Second, you can invite grandparents and other relatives to contribute, perhaps as part of your child's birthday present. Third, kids can help pay for camp themselves by mowing lawns, baby-sitting, or having a paper route. Camp means something more to children who contribute to its cost. For this reason, some families who can pay full price opt to have their children contribute.

  Finally, many community groups and schools sponsor children to attend overnight camp. Talk to your school principal, your clergyman, municipal recreation center leaders, and presidents of community organizations like the Rotary Club. They may be happy to pay part or all of the cost of camp.

Step 6: Conduct personal interviews and inspections.

If you comb through your camp materials with the preceding questions in mind, you should be able to narrow your list of possible camps to five or six. If you end up with more than five or six, be more critical. To help you pick that one best camp from your short list, talk to some parents and children who attended the camps you're considering. If you don't have these personal references already, you can call the directors of the camps you like and ask for names and numbers. While you're at it, you can also interview the camp directors.

Here's our list of the top five questions you should ask each of these sources. Add any other questions you want, and then have the list handy when you call.

Questions to Ask the Camp Director

1.   What is your background and experience in camping?

2.   What is your philosophy of running an overnight camp?

3.   What are the qualifications and training of your staff?

4.   Where do you hire your staff? What percent of them return each summer?

5.   Can you provide me the names and numbers of a few families from your camp who live in my area?

Unless you ask for families in your area, the camp director may give you the names and numbers only of families who were satisfied with their experience. Despite their bias, these folks will be a good source of information. However, asking for camp families in your area forces the camp director to look beyond her personal list of satisfied parents, so you may get a better cross-section of opinions.

Questions to Ask Parents and Kids Who Know the Camp

1.   What did you like most about the camp?

2.   What did you like least about the camp?

3.   What were the other kids like? Do most kids return summer after summer?

4. What were the cabin leaders like at the camp? Do they care about kids?

5. Did you ever go to another camp? Why did you switch?

If you and your child still can't decide which single camp is the best, then call the camps to schedule a visit. Few camps allow unscheduled visits, because they disrupt the daily routine. However, seeing the property first-hand, whether it's during a camp session or during the off-season, makes a memorable impression. You'll learn enough to finalize your decision. With all the information you now have, and all the key questions you've answered, you and your child will be able to pick the camp that suits him best.

Just for kids

How to Watch a Camp Video or CD-ROM

More and more camps use promotional video tapes and interactive CD-ROMs to attract new campers. Here are some tips on how to watch and learn from these media.

1. Remember, the video or CD is an advertisement. It may show you only the most attractive and athletic children, and the best looking equipment and facilities. Is there more to the camp than what's on the video or CD?

2. The best part of the video or CD may be a horse show or a mountain hike that campers had to pay extra money to do. Do all campers get to do all the activities you see on the video or CD?

3. Videos and CDs can make all camps look the same. Pay attention to the small differences between camps. Does the camp have what's important to you?

4. Look carefully at the campers and staff who are featured on the video or CD. This will give you an idea about the mix of kids who go to that camp. Do they seem like kids you would like to have as friends?

5. Listen for whether the narrator describes the cabin leaders and instructors. Where do they come from? Do they like to hang out with kids? Are they nice?

6. Look to see whether the camp seems safe. Are there cabin leaders around to help out the campers, or is everyone running around like crazy? Do you see any safety equipment, such as life preservers?

PART III

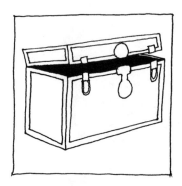

PREPARING FOR CAMP

CHAPTER 8

Emotional preparation and homesickness prevention

*Before I went to camp for the first time, I was nervous. I started thinking,
"What are the other kids going to be like? What if they don't like me? What
if I'm homesick?" I guess most kids are a little nervous before they go to
camp, but it wears off. I mean, I still get butterflies in my stomach when we
drive to camp on opening day, but that's just because I'm excited.*

— Dave, age 13

Homesickness is the distress or impairment caused

by an actual or anticipated separation from home. It's characterized by
acute longing and preoccupying thoughts of home and other beloved
objects. In our research, we found that about 95% of all girls and boys
miss something about home when they're away at camp. In other words,
homesick feelings are normal. Even the adults at camp get a little
homesick. They spend at least nine weeks away from their homes.

Besides being a normal developmental phenomenon, homesickness
also has a silver lining. As a camper once told us, "When you miss home,
it means you love your parents. Plus, you know you've got a lot to look
forward to once you get home."

Some psychologists believe that the homesickness some parents and children feel when they're apart is evidence of the strength of the bond between them. It is comforting to know that love underlies homesickness.

Kids miss all different things when they're away from home. We asked a few hundred campers what they miss most and least when they're at overnight camp. Here's what they told us:

What kids miss most:

1. parents and family
2. friends from home
3. pets
4. boyfriends or girlfriends
5. home cooking
6. junk food
7. television

What kids miss least:

1. school and homework
2. chores and responsibilities
3. sisters and brothers

Homesick feelings are a little different for everyone. One camper might miss his dog the most; another might miss her father's home cooking. Wouldn't it be strange if there wasn't something kids missed about home?

The good news about homesickness

Even though homesick feelings are common, most kids enjoy themselves tremendously at overnight summer camp. On average, kids in our studies rated their camp stay an 8 or 9 on a scale from 0 to 10. No wonder more than seven million kids go away to overnight camp each year. In fact, many return to the same camp year after year.

Fortunately, severe homesickness is rare. In our research, we found that only 1 in 5 children has a bothersome amount of homesickness, and only about 1 in 14 children has a truly distressing degree of homesickness.

Fewer than 1 in 100 kids have to return home early because of severe homesickness.

If you and your child do some simple preparation in the months before opening day, there's an even lower chance that he will experience a bothersome or distressing amount of homesickness. In the next section, we'll outline the best ways to prepare your child for spending time away from home.

In addition, there are lots of things you and your child can do during camp if homesick feelings become bothersome. Campers have told us that the strategies outlined in the *Just for kids* section work especially well. Encourage your child to read that chapter. For parents, we recommend that you implement the anti-homesickness strategies in this chapter and read Chapter 13 to better understand how to respond to a homesick letter from your son or daughter.

Learning to cope with homesickness is a skill your child can use the next time she's away from home. Once children recognize the feeling of homesickness, cope with it, and survive a brief separation from home, their confidence about future separations skyrockets. They really do gain independence, and their self-confidence shapes their attitudes about future separations. Having a confident, positive attitude is one of the best predictors of having a good time at camp. In a way, the cure for homesickness is actually overcoming an initial bout of homesickness. It's like exercise. It may hurt a little, but it makes you stronger. Once your child learns to manage her homesick feelings, she'll have more fun during school trips, sleep-overs, and even freshman year in college.

Can I predict homesickness?

You can roughly predict the strength of homesick feelings by looking at characteristics of your child and the circumstances surrounding her separation from home. As you know, mild homesick feelings are normal. However, the young people who are most likely to experience intense homesickness at camp are those who:

- Have never spent time away from home before
- Feel as if they can't trust other people very much
- Are worried about spending time away from home
- Think that camp is going to be crummy
- Feel forced to go away to camp

The factors above might seem intuitive, but you might be surprised to know that:

- Kids who live far from camp do not get more homesick than kids who live close to camp.

- Kids who don't go to camp with a friend from home are no more likely to have homesick feelings than kids who do go to camp with a friend.

Most kids are pretty good at guessing how strong their own natural homesick feelings will be. If your child is curious, you can get a piece of paper and draw a number scale like the one below. Then, try the following exercise with your child. You might introduce the exercise by saying something like:

> A while ago, you asked me how strong I thought your homesick feelings would be at camp. My guess is that they won't bother you very much, but you're probably better than I at answering that question. Here's a number scale. It's sort of like a thermometer. You can pick any number between 0 and 10, depending on how strongly you feel. For example, if I asked you how much you like to eat liver and onions, you would probably say "0." If I asked you how much you like pizza, you'd probably say "9" or "10." Now you can tell me: On a scale from 0 to 10, how strong do you think your homesick feelings will be at camp?

0	1	2	3	4	5	6	7	8	9	10
not at all strong					**sort of strong**					**very strong**

If your child guessed 0, 1, 2, 3, or 4, say something like: "Your natural homesick feelings probably won't bother you at all while you're at camp. If you happen to think about home, it will probably make you smile."

If your child guessed 5, 6, or 7, say something like: "Your homesick feelings might bother you once or twice. However, if you try hard to have fun, then these feelings won't bother you as much. To get good ideas about having fun at camp, let's read the *Just for kids* section and check out the stuff that camp has sent us in the mail."

If your child guessed 8, 9, or 10, say something like: "Your homesick feelings might get in the way on some days. Maybe not. The good news is that learning how to deal with homesickness, before you go to camp, always makes you feel better. Let's read the *Just for kids* section plus the stuff that camp has sent us in the mail. You'll find lots of helpful hints for having a great time at camp. During some practice time away from home, you can try your favorite anti-homesickness strategies."

Points to Remember about Homesickness

- Homesickness is the distress (usually mild sadness or nervousness) that people feel when they miss home.
- Mild homesickness is normal. Almost all children have some mild homesick feelings when they are away.
- Severe homesickness is rare.
- Talking about homesickness does not cause homesickness, nor make it worse.
- There are many things to think and do before leaving home to lessen homesickness.
- There are even more things to think and do during camp to lessen homesickness.
- Homesick feelings are good in the sense that they reflect the love you have for things at home.
- Homesickness, and getting over it, is a normal process that helps children develop independence and self-confidence.

The best ways to prevent strong homesickness

From our research with thousands of boys and girls, we have discovered techniques that actually work.

1. Include your child in camp planning.

In Chapter 1, we talked about how important it is for kids to feel they have some control over the decision to spend part of their summer at camp. Now you know why. Kids who feel forced to go away are more likely to feel homesick than kids who feel they got to help their parents make decisions about camp. It's important to include your child in the whole process.

2. Talk with your child about homesickness.

Since part of living at overnight camp means parents and children are apart, we think it's a good idea to spend some time together now. In the months before camp starts, find a quiet time with your child and cover the "Points to Remember about Homesickness" from the text box on the previous page. Such a discussion will help educate your child about homesickness, and lay the foundation for the anti-homesickness strategies we outline in the *Just for kids* section.

If you have any difficulty getting a discussion going, try starting with an anecdote of your own experience with homesickness. Alternatively, you might say something like:

> Camp is still a few months away, but I wanted to talk with you about what it's going to be like to be away from home for a while. You'll probably have so much fun that you won't think about home except when you're writing or reading letters. Still, there might be some times when you feel a little homesick, even though you're having a great time. The important thing to remember is that there are lots of things you can think or do to feel better if you feel a little homesick. Most kids have two or three favorite ways of dealing with homesickness. Between now and the start of camp, you can spend some practice time away from home, perhaps the weekend at one of your friends' houses. That will help you figure out what works and what doesn't work for times when you miss home. You can also find out what works best for other kids by reading the *Just for kids* section.

3. Use a wall calendar to plan for camp.

Show your child when camp starts, how long it lasts, and when you'll pick her up. The fewer surprises, the less nervous the whole family will be about camp. We have seen a few campers who arrived at camp pretty stressed out because their parents mixed up which session they were attending. The families went into tailspins when they realized that camp started tomorrow instead of two weeks from tomorrow! As soon as you register, mark Opening Day and Closing Day boldly on your wall calendar.

4. Put the length of stay in perspective.

Kids, especially younger ones, don't have accurate concepts of time. To them, two or four weeks can sound like an eternity. Putting time in perspective is a method of giving them an accurate idea of how long they'll be away from home. This kind of factual preparation often diminishes anxious feelings. There are a couple of excellent ways to help children put time in perspective.

One way to put time in perspective is "marking time." Use the wall calendar on which you've marked the camp dates. Together, count the number of days between Opening Day and Closing Day. Let's say it adds up to 14. Then explain, "OK, here's how long you'll be at camp. That's 14 days. Now let's turn back to this month, where we are now. Find today, and start marking off 14 days. You can cross off today right before you go to bed tonight." Mark the passage of time each day with your child. On the fourteenth day, ask, "How did those two weeks feel? Did it feel like a long time, a short time, or just right?" The answer doesn't matter; it's the mental focus on the passage of time that counts.

A second method of putting time in perspective is "referencing time." By this, we mean referring your child to a memorable time of similar length. For most kids, winter break is a good one. You can say, "Well, you'll be at camp for two weeks, and that's about how long winter break lasted. Did that seem like a long time, a short time, or just right?" Again, your child's answer is not as important as his accurate mental focus on what two weeks feels like.

Putting time in perspective helps kids get a handle on the duration aspect of overnight camp. The more predictable camp seems, the more comfortable it actually is.

5. Re-frame time.

If your child is still nervous after you've helped put her length of stay in perspective, you can try re-framing time. Re-framing time helps children mentally shrink how long their camp stay feels. The easiest way to do this is to help them recall an especially fun time of comparable duration. You might say, "Remember spring vacation? You played outside and we rented videos. Well, that vacation was ten days, and it was over before you knew it. The same thing will happen at camp. Once you start having fun, the time will fly by."

Another way to re-frame time is to say something like, "How many weeks in a year? Right, there are 52. And you're eight and a half years old. So you've been alive for about 450 weeks! That's a lot of weeks. And camp is only two weeks. Two weeks is really not that long, when you consider you're 450 weeks old. Plus, summer vacation is 10 weeks long. Two out of 10 weeks doesn't seem like that much." Re-framing time is a great way to make your child's camp stay seem shorter. It also helps prevent exaggerated statements like, "I'm gonna be at camp forever! Two weeks is practically my whole vacation!"

6. Keep doubts to yourself.

Try not to say things that will make your child worry about how you'll feel when he's away at camp. Sure, you'll miss him, but you've got some interesting things to do while he's at camp, right? Good. Better to say, "Of course I'll miss you, because I love you. But I know you'll have a great time at camp," than to say, "I don't know what I'm going to do while you're gone having a great time at camp. I'm going to miss you so much, but I'll survive somehow." The first sentences convey a positive message and the second ones give your child something to worry about. Leaving home is easier for kids when they know that everything is going to be all right while they're gone.

Deep down, you know your child will have a good time at camp and make it through on her own. Your vote of confidence will mean a lot to her. Remind her how proud you are of her and how she got to help make the decision to go to camp. Tell her that camp will be a fun challenge. If you sense she's anxious, remind her that she's learning things now to help her get the most out of camp.

7. Arrange for practice time away from home.

A long weekend at a friend's house, a stay with grandparents, or a simple sleep-over can help your child get used to being away from home. The more familiar he is with the feeling of separation, the less likely he is to be severely homesick. The key during these dress rehearsals is to simulate, as much as possible, the camp separation. What does that mean? For starters, it means not talking on the phone, since most camps have a no phone call policy. It also means that you, and especially your child, should practice writing a letter or two. After all, that's the primary way you'll stay in touch during camp.

Once your child has completed his practice trip, you can further enhance his ability to deal with homesick feelings. Talk with him about what he could and could not change about the trip, and about the ways he coped with homesick feelings, if he had any. You might say:

- "What were the things about the trip that you could change?" If necessary, prompt your child by saying: "Some examples of things you could change are: how many letters you wrote, what activities you chose to do, and who you talked to about your feelings. What are some other examples of things you could change?"

- "What were the things about the trip you could not change?" If necessary, prompt your child by saying: "Some examples of things you could not change are: how long you were away, what the house rules were, and what the weather was like. What are some other examples of things you could not change?"

- "The best way to deal with any problem, including homesick feelings, is to change the things you can change and then adjust to the things that you can't change." Follow up by asking: "Why do you think this works? Everyone is different. What works best for you?"

- "One of the things you can change when you get to camp is how much you're participating in activities." Follow up by explaining: "In fact, doing a fun activity is the best way to forget about homesick feelings. However, if you feel homesick and you're by yourself, it can be hard to start a fun activity. It's a good idea to find someone else to play with. Doing a fun activity with someone else feels great."

- "For the things that you can't change, try adjusting the way you think about them." Follow up by explaining: "For example, you can't change the number of days that you spend at camp. So try adjusting to that idea. Remember that even though you're away from home for a few days, you'll see me again soon. By the end of the camp session, you may even wish you could stay longer. Thinking that way can make you feel a whole lot better."

8. If possible, avoid moving in the weeks before or during camp.

Overnight camp is usually a comfortable separation. Both parents and kids have fun during their time apart. But too many separations all at once can be uncomfortable. If at all possible, try not to move to a new home in the weeks before or during camp. Moving is stressful partly because it entails leaving old friends and familiar surroundings. Sometimes, having to make new friends at home and at camp, plus getting used to new surroundings at camp and in a new neighborhood, is a lot for kids to handle. Homesickness can result from such huge disruptions. Remember, the fewer worries kids have about how things will go at home while they're away, the better time they'll have at camp.

If you must move around camp time, prepare your child as much as possible. Visit the new home, or look at pictures of it together. Reassure your child that her clothes and toys and other treasured objects will be safely moved. Talk about what her new bedroom will be like, and about the new neighborhood. Answer as many questions about the move as you can to allay her concerns and avoid unpleasant surprises.

9. If possible, avoid traumatic separations in the weeks before or during camp.

We realize that families often cannot control big events like moving. They have even less control over traumatic separations, such as when a husband and wife separate, when a parent leaves for military service, or when a close family member dies. However, sometimes you will have a little bit of control. In those cases, it is best to time the separation in a way that leaves enough days for children to cope with it and ask questions before they leave for camp. Unanswered questions about how family members are doing can shift children's attention from camp to home, leading to stronger homesick feelings.

10. Be truthful about stressful issues.

We recognize that tips 8 and 9 are tough ones. Moving and traumatic separations are sensitive, stressful issues. Above all, remember to be truthful with your child, no matter how poor the timing of a stressful event. Hiding a move or separation from your child, and then doing it behind her back while she is at camp, can be devastating. Parents who do this have good intentions. They think they are shielding their kids from stress. Temporarily, they are. But when the kids return home, they are shocked with a new living situation. Worse, they become mistrustful of their parents and fearful of spending time away from home. They think, "What's going to happen next time I leave home?"

11. Provide comfort to your child after negative life events.

Sometimes, kids experience something scary, stressful, sad, or painful in the months before camp. Maybe their goldfish dies; maybe they change schools; maybe their best friend moves away; maybe their science project bombs; or maybe their parents get divorced. If something is causing your child to be upset, talk about it before she leaves for camp. Kids who discuss and work through negative events before camp have an easier time concentrating on positive events during camp.

Our research has shown that recent negative life events do not necessarily lead to homesickness. In other words, kids who endure a negative event before camp have as good a chance of enjoying overnight camp as other kids. However, we see a few kids every summer whose thoughts during camp linger on something that happened at home before they left. These are probably the kids who didn't have enough time to process the stressful event before they came to camp. Therefore, we recommend that parents make a special effort before camp to help their kids deal with any recent negative life events.

In the rare instance that something bad happens during your child's camp stay, wait to tell him when you see him, at the end of the session. Writing bad news in a letter upsets kids at a time when you cannot provide comfort. Visiting camp in the middle of the session to share some bad news is even more upsetting and disruptive. If a true tragedy occurs and you must immediately be with your child, call the camp director and arrange for your child to return home early.

12. Send your child a letter at camp before the first day.

Getting mail makes kids feel loved and remembered. Personal letters and postcards from parents, friends, and relatives renew the connection with home. Even pets can write letters, with the help of their owners. It's an especially wonderful feeling when mail arrives on the first day of camp. To make this work, you can either mail your letter a few days before opening day, or bring your first letter to camp and give it to your child's cabin leader. The cabin leader can then hand-deliver it on the first full day of camp.

13. Do not make deals about early pick-ups.

Making pick-up deals is an innocent but destructive attempt to reduce pre-camp anxiety. It's normal for children to feel nervous and excited as camp time approaches. It's also normal for first-year campers to be worried about homesickness and ask themselves whether camp is such a good idea in the first place. Unfortunately, some well-meaning parents will try to comfort their child by saying something like, "Well, if you still feel homesick after three days, I'll come to camp and pick you up." This promise almost guarantees that the child will be homesick, and that the parent will be forced to fulfill the promise. What's worse, the child will not gain independence or self-confidence. He may even feel like a failure.

There are two reasons why pick-up deals usually backfire. First, the deal contains a negative message. That message is: "Mom and Dad don't think you can make it through camp. We think that you will be so homesick that the only solution will be to leave camp." The second reason these deals backfire is that they give children a powerful, home-related thought to dwell on: The Pick-Up. Then, every time the child encounters a stressful situation at camp, or feels a twinge of homesickness, his thoughts turn to The Pick-Up. "My parents said that if I didn't like camp, they'd come to pick me up." This thought becomes a mental crutch. The child leans on it, instead of on his own developing power to cope.

Phone deals are equally frustrating for campers and staff. For example, we have sat with campers for hours and comforted them while they told us over and over how their parents promised them they could call home. Apparently, some parents promise phone contact to their children even though the camp makes it clear in its information packet that campers are not allowed to use the phone. You can see how these deals, especially the ones that attempt to break the camp's rules, undermine children's independence and ability to cope.

If your child does ask you, straight out, "Mom, will you come pick me up if I get really homesick and hate camp?" the best answer is something like, "You sound a little nervous about going to camp. But I think you're really going to love it. It's normal to feel nervous before you go. Plus, even if you do have some homesick feelings at camp, you'll know what to think and do to make things better. We're going to learn some strategies that help a lot with homesickness. So, even though you might have some homesick feelings, I think you're going to have a great time at camp."

There is one caveat: Camp is not a jail. Every once in a great while, the best thing for a child is to return home early. Naturally, skilled cabin leaders first work hard with such children to help them cope. Yet, if the child's distress is severe and long-lasting, staff should recognize when the benefits of going home outweigh the benefits of staying at camp. Because decisions about shortening a child's stay at camp are complex, parents and camp staff need to make the decision together. Near the end of the book, we explain how to make this collaborative decision wisely, if you ever come to that rare point.

There you have it—the most powerful ways that parents can help prevent distressing homesickness. Remember, having some homesick feelings before camp or during camp is normal. It also reminds kids of what they love about their home and family, and motivates them to learn valuable coping skills.

Checklist

❑ Include your child in camp planning, so he has a sense of control.

❑ Talk with your child about homesickness, so he understands it's normal.

❑ Use a wall calendar to plan for camp and avoid unpleasant surprises.

❑ Put length of stay in perspective, to help your child grasp the duration of camp.

❑ Re-frame time, to make the camp stay seem relatively short.

❑ Keep doubts to yourself, so you don't make your child more anxious.

❑ Arrange for practice time away from home, so you and your child get used to being apart for a while.

❑ If possible, avoid moves and traumatic separations in the weeks before or during camp.

❑ Be truthful about stressful issues, to instill trust in your child.

❑ Provide comfort to your child after negative life events, so he's less worried while at camp.

❑ Send your child a letter at camp before the first day.

❑ Do not make deals about early pick-ups. This undermines kids' confidence and sets them up for failure. Encourage them instead.

CHAPTER 9

Parents' feelings about camp

Last summer was the first time that Owen had ever spent more than a day away from home. I kept thinking to myself, "He's 9 years old. He'll be just fine at camp." And then I'd think, "He's only 9 years old! Will he be fine at camp?" —Teodora, Owen's mom

For me, the best thing was to talk with other parents who had already sent their kids to camp. It was very reassuring to know that they worried about the same things I did. —Brendan, Michelle's dad

I worried because we didn't get any letters for almost 10 days. I finally had to call camp and talk to Louise's cabin leader. She promised me that Louise was having a great time, which explains why she didn't have the impulse to write. —Gin, Louise's mom

The personal testimonies above are true. A lot of

parents get childsick when their son or daughter is at camp. Of course, all parents enjoy the free time they have while their kids are away, but sometimes that freedom feels empty. Parents miss their kids just like kids miss their parents. It's not always easy to spend a few weeks apart, especially if it's the first time your child has been away from home.

If you're like most parents, you have mixed feelings. You want your child to have a great time at camp, but you're nervous about whether she'll be OK on her own. Without a doubt, reading this book and carefully selecting a camp together will go a long way toward reducing any nervousness. The time you spend now is an investment in your child's happiness. But let's face it. It's normal to be a little nervous when you're not personally there to supervise your child. For those parents who have children with special needs, the separation may be even more difficult. No one knows your child better than you do. How could they? What camp staffs do know is how to keep kids safe and happy. They know how to run a camp.

In this chapter, we'll give you tips to help you enjoy yourself while your son or daughter is at overnight camp. If you don't have any concerns right now, skip this chapter. You can always return to it.

Camp works

Parents tell us that they know camp works because they see positive changes in their children's behavior. It will be interesting to see exactly what you notice when your son or daughter returns home. Of course, just knowing how valuable camp is will not keep you from being concerned. Let's take a look at the research.

A few years ago, we studied parents' anxiety about their kids' going to camp. Several hundred parents were asked to rate how much they agreed with statements such as, "Summer camp is good for children," and "When I am away from my child, I feel lonely and miss him a lot." Almost all parents strongly agreed with the following statements:

- Summer camp is good for children.

- Children learn important social and athletic skills at summer camp.

- My child will benefit from group experiences since they will provide him with social experiences that he could not get at home.

- It is good for my child to spend time away from me so that she can learn to deal independently with unfamiliar people and new situations.

- Children are happy and have fun at summer camp.

No surprises, right? Sounds like a confident group of parents who know what's good for their kids and who recognize the value of camping. No doubt you agree with these statements, too. But don't worry, you're not alone in your concern either. The very same parents also agreed with statements like the following:

- I miss my child when I am away from him.

- When I am away from my child, I often wonder whether she is all right.

- Hugging my child makes me feel so good that I really miss the physical closeness when I'm away.

It's normal, then, to experience a combination of wanting your child to go to camp and being concerned about her well-being. There are two important things to remember about these mixed feelings. First, avoid expressing them to your child. Instead, strive to convey a uniformly positive message about camp. Your child needs your absolute confidence. Second, learn ways to cope with your concern or anxiety.

If only it were that simple, right? In reality, it can be a challenge to manage your strong feelings about your child's going away to overnight camp. But it's not impossible. Let's examine the two solutions.

How can I avoid expressing mixed feelings?

Some of your concern or ambivalence about overnight camp will eventually rub off on your child. He will sense that you're nervous, and that will make it harder for him to feel good about leaving for a few weeks. He may have started out feeling just fine about going to overnight camp, but then he hears you say how worried you are. He thinks to himself, "Well, if my mom and dad are worried, maybe I should be worried too. There must be something scary about camp. Otherwise, my parents wouldn't be worried."

Kids are constantly looking to their parents for guidance on how to feel. This is especially true about new challenges. Remember your child's first steps? He wasn't looking at his feet the whole time. He was looking up at you; looking for your approval and encouragement. That's what he needs now, as he heads off to overnight camp: approval and encouragement.

On the left side of the following table, you'll read some mixed messages that parents sometimes give about overnight camp. On the right side of the table, you'll read a child's probable response to each statement. After each example of a not so good statement, you can read a better alternative statement. These examples should help you clarify what to say and what not to say to your future camper.

Some "not so good" and "better" ways to express your feelings about overnight camp:

Parent says:

not so good:
"Have a great time at camp, Chris. I don't know what I'll do without you."

better:
"Have a great time at camp, Chris. I'm so excited for your adventure."

not so good:
"You'll love camp, Chris. Of course, I'll be bored to tears."

better:
"You'll love camp, Chris. While you're gone, I'll be busy with work and seeing my friends."

not so good:
"These activities sound great. I really should just go to camp with you."

better:
These activities sound great. They're just perfect for kids like you."

Child thinks:

I shouldn't go to camp because my parents may not survive without me.

I should go to camp. My parents will be fine at home without me.

It's not fair for me to go to camp because my parents will be bored without me at home.

I don't have to worry about my parents while I'm at camp. They have lots of their own activities planned.

This camp is for grown-ups, not for kids. I wonder whether I'll like it at all.

Camp is a special place for kids. I bet I'll love it. I wonder what activity will be my favorite?

Parent says:

not so good
"Overnight camp is a good idea, but this is the first time you've been away from home. I sure hope it works out."

better
"Overnight camp is a good idea. Even though this is your first time away from home, I'm sure you'll do fine."

not so good:
"I'm sure everything will be fine. It's just going to make Mommy and Daddy very sad to see you go."

better:
"I'm sure everything will be fine. Of course Mommy and Daddy will miss you...we love you! But we'll see you again really soon."

not so good:
"Three weeks sounds perfect, but that is a mighty long time. I sure hope you can make it that long."

better:
"Three weeks sounds perfect. That's just a little longer than winter vacation, and you remember how short that seemed."

not so good:
"I loved camp when I was a kid, but my God was I ever homesick."

better:
"I loved camp when I was a kid. Of course I missed home a little. That's normal. But I went back to camp for six summers in a row."

Child thinks:

Uh-oh. I thought I could make it at camp, but my parents don't think so. Maybe I just shouldn't go. It might not work out.

This is a new experience but my parents have a lot of confidence in me. If they think I can do it, then I bet I can.

I'm hurting my parents by going to overnight camp. Things that hurt my parents are bad, so overnight camp must be bad, too. Am I bad?

My parents will miss me, but that's not a bad thing. They love me, and they want what's best for me. I'll see them soon.

Three weeks is a mighty long time. I don't think I can make it that long. Better not go.

Three weeks isn't that long, when you think about it. Overnight camp will be just a little longer than winter vacation. I can do it.

Camp is good. No, wait, camp is bad. I'm going to be really homesick, just like my dad.

It's normal to miss home. Even my parents missed home when they went to camp, but you can miss home and still have a fun time at camp. I can't wait to go!

How can I cope with my concern or anxiety?

It's not always easy to hide your concern and mixed emotions. However, there are lots of things you can do to feel better about sending your child to overnight camp. Then you won't have to hide anything. You can simply express how positive you feel. You may always have a bit of concern in the back of your mind, but that's okay.

1. Learn more about your camp.

We advocate learning about camps for many reasons. First and foremost, the more you learn, the better chance you'll have of choosing the best camp for your child. We also advocate learning about camps because the process will decrease any apprehension you have—apprehension caused by not knowing the truth, or not having all the facts. If some aspect of camp remains unknown after you've inspected the camp's materials and talked to other families, don't hesitate to call the director. Lingering questions generate anxiety, so find out what you need to know, and then relax.

2. Talk with other camp parents.

It helps to talk with other camp parents. Knowing that you're not alone in your concern or anxiety is comforting. Parents who have already sent their kids to overnight camp can tell you about their experience. They can help you think positively by telling you about the benefits of overnight camp. They may even have some new ideas for managing your childsickness. If you don't personally know other parents whose kids have gone to overnight camp, then call the camp you chose. As we mentioned in Chapter 7, some camps have a referral list of parents who enjoy talking with other parents. This can be a source of social support and a powerful way to allay your fears. Believe us, most of the parents of the seven million kids who go to camp each year enjoy the time when their kids are at camp.

3. Prepare your child for cabin life.

It's natural to have concerns about how well your child will adjust to living with a large peer group. Every parent knows how small disagreements ("He's touching me!" "She's on my side!" "That's mine!"

"He started it!") can mushroom into a war between two kids. It may be hard to imagine how your child can cope with 8 or 10 kids in a one-room cabin with no one's parents around. Here's how you might broach the topic with your future camper:

> Overnight camp is different from home. Here you live with a few other people, but at camp, you might live with ten in the same cabin. All of these kids will be different from you in some way. They will all look, dress, act, and speak differently than you. Some of them will like different games, sports and music than you do. You've got to respect them all if you want to make friends. Of course, you don't have to be everybody's best friend. You don't even have to like all the other kids. But you do have to try getting along with everyone.

At this point, you might ask your son or daughter for suggestions about the best ways to respect and get along with others. Keep prompting for more suggestions, and then add your own ideas, until you've covered these key points:

- **Treat others fairly.** The Golden Rule is: Treat other people the way you want them to treat you.

- **Cooperate.** Work with your cabin mates, not against them. Lend a helping hand. Listen to your cabin leader.

- **Be a good sport.** Play fairly, follow the rules, and remember to congratulate the other team with a handshake or a camp cheer.

- **Use good manners.** All campers and staff appreciate pleases and thank yous. Make more room for your cabin mates by keeping your elbows off the dinner table.

- **Do your share of the work.** Participate in cabin clean-up, clearing the dinner table, and other cabin chores.

- **Keep your stuff in order.** Small cabins feel crowded when they're messy. Check out Chapter 11 for great packing tips.

- **Care for camp property.** Treat equipment with care, so that others may enjoy it after you. Tell a cabin leader if something is broken. Conserve plants and other nature.

- **Respect other kids' privacy.** Give your cabin mates some space, especially when they're changing. Always knock before opening a door. Use safe touch. (See page 134.)

- **Ask before you borrow things.** Most kids say "yes" to

simple requests if you ask first. While you're using someone else's gear, treat it like your own.

- **Use your words.** Any disagreement can be solved by talking it out. Physical violence is never tolerated at camp.
- **Talk with your cabin leader.** Whether it's good or bad, your cabin leader wants to know what's up. Tell your leader what's going OK and what's not. If there's a big problem in the cabin, ask your cabin leader to arrange a cabin meeting so you and your cabin mates can work together to solve the problem.

4. Stay busy.

Make plans for the time your son or daughter will be at camp. Maybe you'll just have some quiet time alone. Or, if you have other children at home who are not going to camp, this will give you some precious individual time with them.

Some families enjoy planning weekend vacations while their children are at camp. Just give the camp a phone number where you or a family friend can be reached, if needed. Other families have the time and money to take week-long vacations. When children are living at home, it's rare for adults to have child-free time, so seize the opportunity if you can.

If you must continue your usual routine while your child is at camp, at least stay busy in little ways. See friends, go out to the movies, or tackle some project you've been putting off. If you stay busy, missing your child won't bother you much. Of course you'll think about him, and of course you'll miss him. But overnight camp is an important growth experience for him. Think positively and stay busy.

5. Get some news from your child's cabin leader.

When we were cabin leaders, we especially enjoyed parents who devised creative ways to keep in touch. Keeping in touch with us—the cabin leaders—was a comfort to our campers' parents. In addition to handing us letters for their child on opening day, some parents would hand us stamped postcards addressed to them. "Send me a note in a day or two," they would say. "I'd just like to hear how things are going." Using this method, it's a cinch for your child's cabin leader to update you on how things are going at camp. The news will put your mind at ease.

6. Write often.

Renewing contact with your child feels good, so write to her often. She'll love hearing from you. For you, camp may seem close, but for kids, camp can seem as distant as the moon. It's strange, different, and far, far away from home. Make it seem closer by staying in touch. Later on, we'll give you some tips on writing positive letters and responding to signs of homesickness. Just remember: children are not good correspondents. Your child will deeply appreciate every letter you send, but she may not return more than one or two.

7. Take care of yourself.

Relax. Take a bath. Read. Walk. Sleep. Visit a friend. Your child is having a great time at camp. Why shouldn't you enjoy your time at home? Some parents have told me that they feel guilty about having a good time while their child is away at camp. Don't. He hasn't gone away to fight a war or elope or sail around the world alone. (Not yet, anyway.) No, he's not doing anything dangerous or sneaky. He's at an overnight camp with plenty of supervision and fun activities to do. So take care of yourself. Enjoy the time apart. And, when camp is over, enjoy the time back together.

Checklist

❑ Avoid expressing mixed feelings about camp.

❑ Learn about your child's camp.

❑ Talk with other camp parents.

❑ Prepare your child for cabin life.

❑ Stay busy.

❑ Get some news from your child's cabin leader.

❑ Write often.

❑ Take care of yourself.

CHAPTER 10

Physical and medical preparation

0700h-*Thad Tisall. Patient complains of mild abdominal pain. Says he had trouble sleeping last night after eating approx. 17 toasted marshmallows. Gave 2 tablespoons antacid and asked him to take it easy at breakfast. Told to return if pain persists or worsens.* —from a camp health log, 1999

With the possible exception of a few camps with a narrow artistic or academic focus, every overnight camp involves intense physical activity. For that reason, your child's physical health is important. Proper physical and medical preparation is the key to staying healthy at camp. In this chapter, we'll tell you how to physically and medically prepare your child for a fun and healthy stay at overnight camp. You'll find answers to the most frequently asked questions about hygiene, allergies, asthma, and medication-free periods (drug holidays). The chapter concludes with tips for teaching your child about safe and unsafe touch.

Start with the camp health form

Any reputable camp will require a health form that details each camper's medical history. Your report on the camp's health form must be thorough and accurate. Pay special attention to the emergency contacts and immunization sections. In the unlikely event of a serious injury or illness that requires emergency care, camp doctors and nurses will refer immediately to your child's health form. You must also sign the form to give your consent to the camp's health care staff to treat your child. The camp may return the form to you if it is unsigned.

Completing the health form usually requires getting a thorough physical exam from a family doctor or nurse practitioner. A physical exam helps determine whether there are some activities, places, or conditions at camp that might be unhealthy for your child. At the physical exam, the doctor can also refill any prescriptions for medications that your child might need while at camp, such as allergy medication or asthma inhalers. Remember: Bring the health form with you to the physical exam, and be sure the doctor or nurse signs it.

Focus on fitness

Most camp programs keep kids physically active, within the limits of any disability or weight problem they may have. Fortunately, most kids are physically active enough on their own to be in shape for overnight camp. Your child doesn't need to be an Olympic star. However, she should increase her physical activity in the weeks prior to camp. It's enough for most kids simply to spend more time outside doing what they like to do. Kids who spend a lot of time watching television and playing video games will need more time to get in shape. Even if the camp you choose is not very competitive, your child will enjoy it more if she can keep up with the other kids.

To get the most out of a specialty sports camp, your child may want to brush-up on skills before heading to camp. This is easy to do for something like basketball specialty camp. There are hoops and basketballs in most neighborhoods. It's more difficult for something like tennis camp because there may not be a tennis court nearby. And it's nearly impossible to do for something like sailing specialty camp, unless your family owns a boat. Of course, some kids choose a specialty camp because they are beginners and want to learn more, or try something new. In that case, reading a book or magazine about the specialty sport is best.

Swim Checks

Camps that have an aquatics program usually require some type of swim check within 24 hours of the campers' arrival. Swim checks usually consist of swimming a short distance (maybe 50 yards) and treading water for a minute or two. Sometimes the swim check also involves putting a life preserver on in the water or learning to use basic safety equipment. For non-swimmers and children with disabilities, the swim check requirements are appropriately modified.

Whatever the case, it's a good idea for kids to practice swimming before camp starts. Why? Because the swim checks are used to place campers in different levels of lessons. Usually, different levels have different privileges. For example, beginner swimmers may not be allowed to swim in deep water, jump off the diving boards, use certain boats, or go water-skiing.

Obviously, your child will want to do as well in the swim check as she can. We've talked to many campers who were disappointed about the level in which they were placed at the swim check. Like most kids, these campers hadn't had much chance to swim recently, so they didn't do as well in the swim check as they might have. A little practice at a local pool before coming to camp would have helped them do better. Don't despair if there's nowhere to practice. Most camps with aquatics programs offer swim lessons. Your child may move up a level in swimming, and get more privileges, just by going to a few lessons early in the camp session.

Teach proper hygiene

It's a simple idea: Preventing illness keeps kids healthy, and when they're healthy, they have much more fun at overnight camp. What can kids do to reduce the chance that they'll get sick at overnight camp? Here's a comprehensive list made by two experienced camp nurses. We've added a few details. This list is useful, not just for the time children spend at overnight camp, but for all the time, and for all family members.

High quality cabin leaders will assist children in following these simple guidelines for healthy living. However, you should give your child practice following these guidelines before he arrives at camp. Kids owe it to themselves and to their cabin mates to keep themselves as healthy as possible.

- Wash your hands with soap and water before eating, after using the toilet, and whenever they look dirty. Don't forget to scrub underneath your fingernails.

- Shower or swim each day to keep your body clean. In the shower, use shampoo, soap, and hot water.

- Brush and floss your teeth at least once a day.

- Turn your head and cover your mouth and nose when coughing or sneezing. Use tissues or handkerchiefs whenever possible.

- Don't share food, utensils, toothbrushes, combs, or other personal items.

- Dress appropriately for the weather. If it's cold and rainy, wear clothes that are warm and dry.

- Change your clothes (especially socks and underwear!) each day.

- Change your sheets and pillow cases each week. If you wet or soil your bed or sleeping bag, tell a cabin leader so that it can be cleaned.

- Air out your sleeping bag each week, if you use one.

- Put on sunscreen and a hat before spending time in the sun. Reapply sunscreen after swimming or exercise.

- Wear supportive shoes and thick socks, not sandals, for long hikes.

- Eat balanced meals.

- Drink at least one full glass of water at each meal, in addition to other fluids, such as milk and juice. Between meals, use the drinking fountains around camp.

- Sleep eight hours each night.

- At night, use a flashlight when walking around camp.

- Find outlets for stress, such as exercise, relaxation techniques, or a mid-day rest.

(*Source: Lishner & Bruya*, Creating a Healthy Camp Community, *1994*)

Sometimes, health issues at camp embarrass kids. If their bodies aren't clean, they may smell. If their underwear is dirty, they may itch in private places. If they wet their sleeping bag or bunk bed, they may be worried about telling their cabin leader. These things might make your child feel uncomfortable, but it's better to be embarrassed for a moment than to get sick for a day or more. Encourage your child to ask his cabin leader if he needs a little help cleaning up.

For Young Women

Moms and dads should discuss menstruation with their daughters before camp. You never know exactly when your daughter may have her first period, and you want her to be prepared for this natural occurrence. If you discuss menstruation and how to use a pad or a tampon before camp starts, then you can avoid any major discomfort or embarrassment during camp. An excellent book about the topic is *Before She Gets Her Period: Talking to Your Daughter About Menstruation*, by Jessica B. Gillooly, Ph.D.

Teach proper medical self-care

There are two medical things your child should know before she goes to overnight camp. First, if she takes medicines, she should know what they are for and how to take them. Second, she should know a little bit about first aid for very minor injuries.

It is an ACA standard, and a law in many states, that both prescription and non-prescription medicines at camp be kept under lock and key. Most often, medicines are locked up at the camp's health center. Camps do this to prevent children from accidentally taking too much or the wrong medication. Some exceptions are sunscreen, bug repellent, asthma inhalers, and EpiPens®. Camps do allow kids to keep these products with them. Because medicines are kept locked up, most camps have a scheduled time when campers who take medicine are supposed to come to the health center or infirmary. For example, there might be a "med call" before and after mealtime. Because camp staff won't always remind your child to take his medicine, he needs to learn proper medical self-care.

Kids should know why they take the medicine they do. Understanding why they take medicine helps them remember to take it. We've met a surprising number of children who know nothing about the medicine they take each day. They've told us things like, "It's my pill. I take one every day." Their parents and doctors have kept them in the dark. Naturally, these kids sometimes forget to take their pills because they don't know why they should. To parents who have already taught their child why he takes a certain medicine, bravo! There's a much better chance your child will remember to take his medicine at camp if he understands why it's important.

Many kids with complex medication regimens, such as those with diabetes or cancer, know exactly what they take, why they take it, and when they need it. Other kids with complex medical issues attend special medical needs camps to learn more about caring for themselves.

All kids with medical issues—complex or otherwise—should go with their parents to meet the camp nurse or doctor on opening day. You and your child should prepare for that meeting now. Meet with your health care provider and discuss any changes in your child's self-care regimen. Be sure that the medication schedules and procedures are clarified before going to camp. As a general rule, the less you deviate from your home-based or hospital-based medication schedule, the better.

One crucial fact all campers must know about medicine is: Never accept medicine from another camper under any circumstances. At camp, only the camp nurse or doctor should be dispensing medicine.

Every camper should know a few things about basic first aid. For example, your child should know how to clean a small cut, put on an adhesive bandage, and change that bandage once a day, or more often if it becomes wet or dirty. She should also know that any strong pain, swelling, or persistent bleeding means go see the camp nurse or doctor. Of course, basic and advanced medical care at camp is the responsibility of the staff, not the campers. Nevertheless, you'll feel more comfortable sending your child to overnight camp when she knows first aid for things like bleeding and choking. Your local American Red Cross teaches basic first aid courses just for kids.

A Camper's Basic First Aid Kit

- selection of adhesive bandages
- small packet of facial tissues
- anti-itch cream or stick
- antibacterial cream
- sunscreen (minimum SPF 15)
- insect repellant
- zippered plastic sandwich bags (for disposal of used bandages)

Second to sunburn, the most common minor injury kids get at camp is a bug bite. One strategy against bug bites is prevention, but it's a nuisance. Bug repellent works well, but you have to remember to use it. You also have to remember to reapply it after swimming or exercise. Once kids have bites, they tend to scratch them, sometimes until they bleed. Like any cuts or scrapes, these small open wounds are breeding grounds for germs and can lead to infection. Instead of scratching, we recommend using After Bite® or another anti-itch preparation, such as Benadryl® cream or hydrocortisone cream. They work well to stop itching and are a good addition to any camper's first aid kit.

Allergies

Many kids have allergies. Some of them are severe, even life-threatening. Others are relatively minor and don't cause anything more than a stuffy nose. The way that you and your child should prepare for camp depends on the severity of the allergy and on the allergen (what your child is allergic to). When kids understand their allergy and how to deal with it, it doesn't keep them from having fun.

Some allergens are easy to avoid. For example, kids allergic to milk can simply avoid milk and milk products. Most camps are happy to provide some alternative, such as rice milk or soy milk. Other allergens are harder to avoid. For example, some kids who are allergic to peanuts must avoid peanuts, peanut butter, all foods made with peanut butter or cooked in peanut oil, and any other foods or utensils that have peanut residue on them. Some people are so allergic to peanuts that they get hives if they eat jelly from a jar into which someone has dipped a peanut-buttery knife. It's not easy to avoid that sort of thing at camp, but kids with serious allergies need to learn how. After you've chosen a camp, talk with the director about your child's allergy before opening day. Find out how the camp and kitchen staff can assist your child in avoiding certain allergens.

Some allergens are impossible to avoid. There are minor ones, such as dust. Kids who are allergic to dust may use nasal sprays or oral medication to avoid congestion and other symptoms. Be sure to bring these medicines to camp. Other allergies that are impossible to avoid can have severe symptoms. For example, kids who are allergic to bees may have trouble breathing after they are stung. Although the camp has an obligation to provide the highest quality treatment to your child in the event of any emergency, kids with severe allergies need to learn how to treat themselves. Before opening day, these kids should practice their response to severe symptoms, such as how to use an EpiPen® or an AnaKit®. When you meet with the camp nurse or doctor on opening day, discuss your child's allergies and allergy medications.

A final note on allergies: Because someone who doesn't know your child's medical history may have to help in an emergency, kids with severe symptoms should wear a MedicAlert® bracelet or necklace. The information on MedicAlert® tags can help an adult respond with the right kind of first aid, should it be necessary.

Asthma

Asthma, which is caused by inflammation or narrowing of the airway, is the most common chronic illness in children. About 4% of U.S. children are affected. Psychological factors, such as anxiety, and environmental agents, such as cold air, can make it worse. The symptoms of an asthmatic episode include wheezing and coughing. Because physical exercise sometimes induces an episode, kids with asthma are usually free to carry inhalers with them around camp. Generally, using an inhaler opens up the airway, and the symptoms go away.

If your child has asthma, be sure he knows how and when to use his inhaler, as well as his other asthma medications. Caring for asthma can be a drag, so consult your health care professional if your child has trouble adhering to his treatment regimen. Bring an extra inhaler to camp for the medical staff to keep, along with a nebulizer if your child uses one. Clearly label the inhalers and other equipment in case it's found somewhere around camp. As with any medical condition, be sure to discuss your child's symptoms and treatment with the camp health center staff and with your child's cabin leader. Kids with mild or moderate asthma generally do fine at any overnight camp. If your child's symptoms are unusually severe, or if he is struggling to cope with the impact of his illness, consider one of the many special needs camps designed for kids with asthma.

Psychiatric medications and medication-free periods

Kids who take psychiatric medications, such as a stimulant or an anti-depressant, should go with their parents, before camp starts, to consult with the psychiatrist who prescribed the medication. Families should also consult with the child's psychotherapist if that person is not the same one who prescribed the medication. These pre-camp consults are important for several reasons.

First, you'll want to make sure that your child has more than enough medication to last the entire camp stay. Camps in remote locations may have difficulty refilling prescriptions if they run out half-way through the camp session.

Second, you'll want to design a medication schedule that fits the camp's daily schedule. At school, medication may be easy to administer every few hours, but at camp, the normal dosing times may fall in the middle of an activity period. Show your child's psychiatrist the camp's daily schedule and discuss a realistic dosing schedule. Before and after meals are convenient times for campers to visit the health center. Switching to a long-acting form of the medication is often the most convenient solution.

Third, kids must know how to recognize and manage any side-effects of their medication. Common side effects like dry mouth, sleep problems, and loss of appetite may worry your child unless he recognizes the symptoms as side-effects of his helpful medication. On opening day, it's also a good idea to give your child's cabin leader a short note explaining possible medication side-effects. If cabin leaders are misinformed, they may mistake the origin of your child's symptoms. For example, they may think his dry mouth means he is dehydrated, or that his loss of appetite is from homesickness. This misunderstanding may lead the cabin leader to address a problem that doesn't exist.

Fourth, you'll want to discuss the possibility of a medication-free period, or "drug holiday." Medication-free periods are set times when doctors and parents plan for kids not to take a certain psychiatric medication. Sometimes medication-free periods work well, but not always. The decision to have a medication-free period during overnight camp needs to be made thoughtfully. Parents and kids should discuss the pros and cons with the treating therapist and with the psychiatrist who prescribed the medication. Here are some of the pros and cons to discuss:

Pro: Overnight camp is intended to be a relaxing, recreational, and supportive environment. At most camps, there are no academic pressures. If your child's psychiatrist was already considering a trial off the medication, camp might not be a bad time to try.

Con: Your child is on his medication for a reason. The hope is that she is currently benefiting from the positive effects of that medication. Taking the medication away removes one of her ways of coping. The camp experience can be made unnecessarily difficult when kids have to deal with everything new at camp plus the experience of stopping some helpful psychiatric medication. The reasons why your child is currently taking a psychiatric medication probably won't disappear at overnight camp, so the medication probably shouldn't either.

Psychiatric medications are long-acting. For example, it can take a week or more for some anti-depressants to get out of your child's system. This fact, combined with the change in environment, makes it hard to look back, after a two-week session at camp, and decide whether the medication-free period was successful or not.

Pro: One of the most popular reasons that doctors and parents plan medication-free periods is to give kids a break from undesirable medication side-effects. This is commonly the case with stimulant medications that are prescribed for attention deficit hyperactivity disorder (ADHD). These medications include Ritalin (methylphenidate), Dexedrine (dextroamphetamine), Cylert (pemoline), and Adderall (mixed amphetamines). Some psychiatrists recommend occasional medication-free periods because these medications may temporarily decrease kids' appetites and growth rates. Some stimulant medications may also temporarily cause drowsiness or depressive symptoms. If your child is experiencing uncomfortable side effects from the medication she takes each day, then it can be relieving to take a break.

Con: Many kids with ADHD who were well-behaved while on medication come to camp during a medication-free period and face huge challenges. These kids did well at school while taking their stimulant medications. They were able to listen and follow directions. They were able to make and keep friends, and they were confident in their abilities. However, things change for these kids when they stop taking their medication and come to camp. Compared to school, camp has just as many times when they have to listen, follow directions, and keep their bodies calm. Off medication, these kids struggle to follow simple directions. Camp also has many new potential friends, but impulsive, hyperactive behavior makes these kids difficult playmates. For these

A Cabin Leader's Perspective on Medicated Children

"At first, I had mixed feelings about having campers on stimulant medications. I remember one boy who became sort of subdued and spacey after taking his meds. Our camp doctor discovered that he was slightly overmedicated, and changed his dose. After that, he was just like any other kid—lively, enthusiastic, and creative. Although you'd never know he had ADHD, I was glad that his parents had clued me in. They told me about the medication's side effects and gave me suggestions for helping him show good behavior."

What does medical research say about these side effects?

Drowsiness is a side effect in about 6% of children on Dexedrine, Ritalin, or Cylert. Confusion or "dopey" behavior occurs in about 10% of children on Dexedrine; about 4% of children on Ritalin; and hardly ever for children on Cylert. Depressive symptoms occur in about 39% of children on Dexedrine, 9% of children on Ritalin, and hardly ever for children on Cylert. These figures are averages and may not reflect your child's response to a medication. Side effects vary according to the medication, the dose, and the individual child. Be sure to consult with the prescribing psychiatrist for the most accurate information about your child.

(Source: Maxmen & Ward, Essential Psychopathology and Its Treatment, *1995)*

social and emotional reasons, many child psychiatrists and psychologists are adamantly against medication-free periods at camp. Stopping an otherwise helpful medication at camp can turn what is supposed to be a fun, relaxing time into a miserable, stressful time.

The Expert Opinion: Russell A. Barkley, Ph.D., a clinical psychologist and world-renowned expert on ADHD, says this regarding medication-free periods:

Treatment can be stopped annually for a week or two, usually a month or so after the beginning of the new academic year to give the child time to get used to the new school year and the teacher to get to know the child before stopping the medicine. When a doctor waits to see if a child who has been off medication for the summer has trouble in school without it, the child is put in the position of developing a bad reputation with the teacher and classmates—

an image he or she must then overcome after going back on the stimulants. We believe it's better to get the school year off to a good start with the medication and then stop the medication briefly during October. If there is a brief decline in school performance, the child can be kept on medication during that school year.

(Source: Barkley, *Taking Charge of ADHD*, 1995)

The conclusion: We agree with Dr. Barkley that the best time to try a medication-free period is a month or so after a child has settled in to a new place and a new routine. For most campers, that means staying on stimulant medications as prescribed because camp lasts less than a month. However, for some kids at 8-week camps, it may be worthwhile trying a medication-free period during the second month of camp. If you do opt for a medication-free period, please tell the camp nurse or doctor so they understand your child's medical history and can monitor his progress for you.

The bottom line is that stimulant medications help most kids with ADHD adjust to change. Therefore, medication-free periods are best attempted after these kids have had a month or so to get used to a new environment. That generally excludes camp as a testing ground.

Teach about safe and unsafe touch

Just like a classroom, a playground, or a friend's house, camp is a place where kids play and talk with adults and other young people. These interactions are usually safe and fun. However, on rare occasions, another child or an adult may use bad judgment. He or she might try something unsafe with your child. Chances are, you've already taught your child basic rules for staying safe around other people. For example, you've told her not to talk to strangers, not to take candy or money from a stranger, and not to get in a car with a stranger. You've also probably told her how to say "no" if another child or an adult offers her drugs. However, not all parents have talked to their kids about safe and unsafe touch. It's a sensitive topic, and it's hard to find the right words. All parents feel a little awkward talking about touch with their kids.

If you've selected a camp thoughtfully, or if you've gotten a camp recommendation from a trusted friend, then there is very little chance of any unsafe situation occurring there. High quality camps hire high quality staffs. The staff at a high quality camp knows how to monitor their own behavior and the behavior of their campers in order to keep everyone safe and happy. However, unsafe touch between two campers, or between a staff member and a camper, is even less likely to occur when kids know the difference between safe and unsafe touch. If you haven't yet talked to your son or daughter about keeping his or her body safe, now is a good time.

Education: What's the difference between safe and unsafe touch?

The first thing you want to do is make sure your child knows the difference between safe and unsafe touch. No one has the right to touch your child on a private place on his body or in a way that makes him feel uncomfortable. There are two aspects of safe touch: where it happens and how it makes you feel.

As far as where it happens, the easiest way to explain unsafe touch to kids is to say, "Unsafe touch is when someone touches a place on your body that is normally covered by your bathing suit. Most other places are safe to touch, as long as it doesn't make you feel uncomfortable." You can give examples, such as, "Safe touch includes pats on the head, high-fives, a hand on a shoulder or back, and brief hugs." You might also explain that during instructional activities at camp, safe touch may include a hand on the stomach to support a novice swimmer, hands on lower legs to position a water-skier, or even hands near the waist to fasten a climbing harness. The bathing suit rule will help you remember that safe touch is different for boys and girls. For boys, safe touch can include pats on the chest during a touch football game. However, for girls, pats on the chest would not be safe touch. For both boys and girls, bathing suits cover their genitals and buttocks. Unwelcome touch in these private areas is unsafe.

How it makes you feel is the other part of safe touch. You can easily explain this to your child by saying, "Safe touches shouldn't make you feel uncomfortable. If someone is touching you in a way that makes you feel uncomfortable, that's unsafe. If it makes you feel uncomfortable, it doesn't matter where the person is touching you. Uncomfortable touch is unsafe." You can give an example, such as, "Someone might pat you on the back for doing a good job. If that feels good, it's safe touch. But if it starts to make you feel uncomfortable, it becomes unsafe touch."

After discussing these and other examples of safe and unsafe touch, your child should be able to recognize safe and unsafe touch based on where the touch is and how it makes him feel. Children should be proud of their bodies, yet understand that private body parts are just that: private.

There is one exception that you should discuss: doctors and nurses sometimes need to touch children's bodies in private places. For example, a thorough physical exam includes a genital exam. Doctors and nurses might also need to touch a child's body in a way that makes him feel uncomfortable. For example, they sometimes need to give children shots. Most young people intuitively understand that doctors' and nurses' professional duties are an exception to the safe touch rules. Still, you should mention this one exception so your child doesn't get confused the next time she goes for a physical exam.

Prevention: How can kids prevent unsafe touch?

Here are some concrete guidelines for preventing unsafe touch that you can give your child. Remember not to talk just about camp, or your child may think that camp is the only place where she needs to be careful. Although unsafe and unwelcome touches are rare, they can happen in any environment. Children should know how to protect themselves wherever they are.

You might start by saying something like, "Bodies are wonderful things. It's amazing if you think about it. There are 6 billion people in the world, and everyone's body is different! Bodies come in all shapes, sizes, and colors. It's important to remember that your body belongs to just one person—you! Here are some ways to keep your body and other people's bodies safe, whether you're at school, at camp, or just sleeping over at a friend's house." After this type of brief introduction, you can share these examples of how to prevent unsafe touch.

- **Don't sit on another person's bed unless you are invited.**
  At camp, at home, and at school, people live together and they learn to share many things. You may even share a bed with your brother or sister at home, but at camp, everyone's bed is his own. It's private space. You don't have to share your own bed, and you need to get permission before you sit on another person's bed.

- **Don't share sleeping bags with anyone.** Your sleeping bag is private space. It's made especially for one person—you. No one should ever share it with you, even on a chilly night. If someone forgets this rule, remind him or her.

- **Don't walk around naked.** Of course, there are some OK times to be naked, such as when you're changing your clothes or when you're taking a shower. Things may be different at home, but elsewhere, there are times when it might bother people if you are walking around naked. For example, when you're at camp and you need to go outside your cabin to hang your wet bathing suit on the clothesline, put on some clothes first.

- **When people are changing their clothes, give them privacy.** Whether they're in their bedroom, a locker room, or a tent at camp, don't touch people who are changing their clothes. Give them some room and wait until they are done changing.

- **When people are showering, give them space.** At some camps and schools, the showers have private stalls. Everyone gets their own little shower. At other camps and schools, all the showers are together in one big room. Even in these big rooms, people need their own private space. Don't touch or stare at someone who is showering.

- **If another kid asks you to stop touching him, you should stop.** You might not think your touch is unsafe, but you should stop anyway. Remember, it's the other kid's body, not yours. He gets to decide what feels comfortable and what doesn't.

This is a good list of tips for kids who are going to camp, but it's not comprehensive. Want to learn more? See *Resources & references* for a list of kids' books about safe and unsafe touch.

Intervention: What should kids do if unsafe touch happens?

Unsafe touch is rare at schools, camps, and other places where there are many adults to supervise each activity. Even though it's rare, your child should still know what to do if someone uses unsafe touch. It doesn't matter whether the unsafe touch was unwanted tickling, pinching, hugging, kissing, rubbing, or fondling. Your child's response should be the same. In these words, or in your own words, discuss these two steps with your son or daughter:

1. **Tell the person to stop.** Remember, your body belongs to you. You always have the right to tell someone not to touch you. No matter who the person is, how nice they are, how old they are, or what they tell you about why they are touching you, it's OK to ask them to stop. Sometimes, people who touch kids in unsafe ways try to convince them that it's OK, but it's not, no matter what. If the touching makes you feel uncomfortable, or if the touching is in a private place, you need to ask them to stop. Say, "Please don't touch me" in a loud, firm voice. Be serious and look the person in the eye. Don't giggle or smile. If the person doesn't stop right away, repeat "Please don't touch me!" in an even louder voice. Move the person's hands off of you, and step away from them.

2. **Tell a trusted adult.** If another child or an adult has touched you in an unsafe way, you must make sure it doesn't happen again. Therefore, it's very important to tell a trusted adult. This could be your cabin leader, another staff member, the camp director, or one of the other adults in charge. If the person who touched you is one of the adults in charge, then you need to tell a different adult. If the first person you tell is busy or doesn't listen, tell someone else. Keep trying until someone listens. Tell exactly what happened and who did it. Remember that if someone touches you in an unsafe way, it is never ever your fault. You won't get in trouble.

Some kids are worried about telling a trusted adult about some unsafe touch that happened. They fear that talking about it will be embarrassing. Or, they fear that telling about it might get someone in trouble. Kids may feel as if they are betraying the loyalty of a person they admire. Emphasize to your child, "It might not be easy to tell a trusted adult, but it is important. First of all, telling a trusted adult will get the person to stop touching you. It will keep your body safe. Telling a trusted adult will also help the person who touched you. That person will get help understanding the difference between safe and unsafe touch. Don't worry at all about hurting anyone's feelings. Your safety is always more important than someone else's feelings. Always."

A Final Note on Touch

Rest assured that high quality camps are extremely safe places, in all respects. Even so, random contact or unwelcome affection can sometimes be misperceived as unsafe touch. Remember that everyone at camp comes from a unique family, with its own culture and traditions. Every family has its own ways of expressing affection, and almost all touch among family members is meant to be affectionate. Therefore, some unwelcome touch is benign.

If your child reports being touched in an unsafe way, that doesn't necessarily mean that he or she has been abused. Praise your child for telling you what happened, but then talk to the camp director before you jump to conclusions or unfairly accuse someone. Of course, the best policy is to prevent unsafe touch in the first place. Your child should know how to ask assertively not to be touched in a way that feels unsafe.

CHAPTER 11

Packing

Don't leave it all to the last minute. Although many

families dread packing, it doesn't have to be a test of wills. If you pack
together, a bit ahead of time, the process can actually be enjoyable. At the
very least, knowing what and how to pack can decrease the chances of
forgetting important equipment or running out of underwear half-way
through the session. Naturally, if you delay packing until the last minute,
it can become a nightmare. No matter how long camp lasts, living out of
a footlocker, suitcase, duffel bag, or backpack takes careful preparation. In
this chapter, we'll provide seasoned commentary about what to pack,
what not to pack, and how to increase the chances that your child will
bring it all home when camp is over.

Start with the camp's list

If you have not received a clothing and equipment list from the camp you
and your child chose, call now and ask for one. This list is important
because it's been developed and refined over several seasons. It's custom-
tailored to fit the regional weather and the unique program of activities at
your particular camp. For example, your child may need blue shorts to
match the camp uniform, dress clothes for a dance, or leather boots for
horseback riding.

Read through the camp's entire list once, so that you know what items
campers require. There may also be a list of optional items that you and

your child should evaluate. Some camps publish a very specific list, and even tell kids how many of each item to bring. Other camps publish a rather general list that says "shirts" without specifying what kind or how many. Once you have an idea about what to pack, set aside the camp's list and return to this chapter to learn the five basic principles of packing for overnight camp. Next, read our commentary on specific items. You can then return to the camp's list with an educated view, help your child make some choices and personal additions, and start packing. Pack together. It demonstrates your enthusiasm about camp, and it ensures he won't forget crucial items.

1. Label everything.

We can't count the number of times one of our campers asked in vain, "Has anyone seen my white socks?" Asking this question is like going to a crowded beach on a hot day and asking whether anyone has seen your towel. The answer is: If you haven't labeled it, there's no hope of getting it back. That's why the first principle of packing is: label everything.

If you visit some camps' waterfronts, athletic fields, or cabins, you'll see a sight reminiscent of tornado damage. Towels, shirts, socks, shoes, and gear will be strewn everywhere. In this kind of chaos, kids forget.

That towel left by the docks will get trampled and rained on before someone (maybe) puts it in the lost-and-found. There, it will begin to mildew and take on the odor of rotten eggs. However, if the towel is labeled, it may find its way back to its owner before meeting such a fate. Labeling might also reduce the chances that an item will be stolen, although theft at camp is generally a minor problem. Still, you should label everything, not just clothes. Label your child's soap case, cassette tapes, sports equipment, hats, and shoes. Label everything!

You have several options for labeling. None of the methods is perfect, but some are easier to use than others. Most families combine methods to suit their needs. Vendors for each can be found in the *Resources & references* section at the end of the book.

- **Indelible Ink Stamps.** This is the best all-around method of labeling. Indelible ink stamps are metal or rubber stamps with

Sock Labeling Tips

At our camp, the laundry service does a pretty good job of folding the clean clothes and stacking them in the laundry bags. Even without labels, many clothes are distinctive enough to be easily identified by their owners when it's time to pass out clean laundry. However, at the bottom of every laundry bag lurks a pile of socks and underwear that every cabin leader dreads.

For some reason, many families forget to label socks, or do so poorly. Also, white cotton socks tend to get stretched and fuzzy, turning D's into O's and M's into blobs.

Sorting out seventy pairs of white socks can be a test of mental endurance. To help your child and his cabin leader, use a laundry marking pen and invent a simple but distinctive code or design for the socks, such as two circles "••", a double dagger "‡" or a big S and little t "St" if your last name is something like Smith. Such distinctive marks can be identified and matched up quickly. Put the label near the toe so the symbol doesn't show when your child wears his shoes.

your child's name, usually in capital letters. When you order an indelible ink stamp, ask for both first and last names, or at least first initial and last name. Otherwise, two children with the same last name might get their stuff mixed up. Indelible ink stamps work especially well on clothes. Stamp shirts inside the collar, pants and underwear inside the waistband, and socks on the top of the toes. Stamp other items in a logical but inconspicuous place. Don't stamp an item in an obscure spot or no one will be able to find the name.

- **Laundry Marking Pens.** Laundry marking pens are made especially for labeling clothes, but you can also use them to label plastic, metal, leather, graphite, and wooden items, such as soap boxes, canteens, baseball gloves, tennis racquets, and lacrosse sticks. Laundry marking pens have the advantage of being quick and easy to use, but they can fade and distort with repeated washing or use. Therefore, it's a good idea to actually pack one to use for re-labeling at camp. The Sanford "Rub-a-Dub"® is a good laundry marking pen and is available at most office supply stores. Whatever the brand, be sure to use a laundry-proof marking pen, not a simple waterproof pen. There is a difference.

- **Iron-On / Sew-On Labels.** These labels are strips of fabric with your child's name printed on them. Iron-on labels are faster to apply than sew-on labels, but they tend to peel off if not applied correctly, or if ironed on an item that is frequently stretched or abraded. Therefore, we recommend iron-on labels for shirts, shorts, and pants, but not for socks. Use a laundry marker or stamp for socks.

    Sew-on labels are usually permanent, but they take a long time to apply. The average camper needs more than 60 different items of clothing, which would take hours to label with sew-ons. Therefore, if you use sew-on labels, we recommend you reserve them for expensive items, such as jackets, or for clothing made out of artificial fabrics, such as Gore-Tex®, that don't take iron-ons well or that may be damaged by the heat of an iron.

2. Wash and wear before camp.

Almost all families will need to buy a few new items of clothing to complete their camp packing list. Whether it's socks, shoes, or a T-shirt, we recommend that kids wash and wear all new items of clothing before packing them. Washing and drying clothes causes them to shrink. Even if the shrinkage is minimal, kids should still make sure that all their clothes fit before packing them. It's upsetting to realize, after you get to camp, that all your socks are too small or that your new T-shirt comes up to your belly button.

For items that are not normally washed, such as shoes, boots, and rain coats, we recommend that kids wear them around before opening day to break them in and spot any defects. Getting blisters from a stiff pair of new shoes, or realizing during the first thunderstorm that your new rain coat doesn't have a hood, can ruin an otherwise fun day at camp.

3. Prepare for losses.

Camp can be brutal on clothing and other gear. Things get wet, muddy, stretched, torn, borrowed, abused, stuffed in corners, and lost for days. Therefore, we recommend that kids don't bring expensive clothing and gear to overnight camp unless they are mentally prepared for the possibility of never again seeing it. This is not meant to worry you. Most kids don't lose much, and theft is rare, but it does happen. If a shirt gets put in the wrong laundry bag and winds up in a different part of camp, it may never find its way home, even if it's labeled.

Granted, the clothing your child brings should be decent quality. It has to be good enough to survive hiking up a mountain, sliding into second base, falling in a football game, and stretching during capture-the-flag. Nevertheless, you shouldn't go overboard on quality. Whatever your child brings will probably get dirty, maybe permanently. Many camps use cold water wash cycles followed by industrial-strength dryers that generate volcanic heat. The combination gets clothes mostly clean, but then bakes in the remaining dirt and stains.

All kids want to fit in with their fellow campers, and fashionable clothing can be a big part or a small part of fitting in, depending on the camp. But camp is not a fashion show. Your child can be fashionable without having to be a supermodel. Steer clear of camps where brand names seem essential. That kind of superficiality is the opposite of what overnight camp is supposed to be about. In response to this issue, some camps require simple uniforms, such as blue shorts and T-shirts. For other camps, you should pack fashionable, functional clothing, but not if that requires you to bring a $250 cashmere sweater. Remember, this is overnight camp. Prepare for a few losses.

4. Consider laundry frequency.

You can determine how many of each clothing item to pack based on the frequency of the laundry service. If the camp's information packet doesn't say, call and ask. For camps that last a week or less, there probably isn't any laundry service, so your child should pack enough clothes to last $1^1/_2$ times the number of days she'll be at camp. For example, if it's a six-day camp, pack nine days worth of clothes, just to be on the safe side.

Camps that last more than a week usually have a laundry service. To figure out how much clothing your child should bring, calculate the number of days between laundry services and multiply that number by 1.5. For example, if laundry is done once every seven days, pack enough clothing to last 7 x 1.5 days, or 10.5 days. That formula gives your child some extra clothes in case the laundry service is delayed or some of her clothes get wet and don't have a chance to dry out. Kids who think they will change outfits more than once a day, because of certain activities or because they sweat a lot, should pack even more extra clothes.

5. Pack in the recommended container.

Campers need to pack all their clothes and gear in some type of container. This could be a footlocker or trunk, a suitcase, a duffel bag, or a large backpack. The camp information packet should specify the preferred container. If not, call the camp and ask. You should follow the camp's recommendation because they know the space limitations of the living quarters and whether closets, drawers, or lockers are available.

Trunks or footlockers are favorite containers at camp because they are tough, compact, and easy to organize. Trunks also double as card tables, chairs, and step-ladders to top bunks. Like everything else, trunks range in quality. The worst ones are no better than a flimsy cardboard box. Trunks are readily available at discount department stores, army surplus stores, and through outdoor supply catalogs. You may also be able to borrow one or find one in the attic, perhaps a relic from military service or your own childhood camping experience. Newer versions are made of plastic, but some are less sturdy than particle board, plywood, or metal. If a trunk sags when your child stands on it, then it probably won't last very long at camp, where it will be bumped, stepped on, stacked, and dropped.

If your camp offers a choice of what to pack clothes and gear in, consider what your child will do with that container. If he's taking an airplane to camp, it's easier to bring a suitcase, especially one with wheels, than it is to haul around a trunk. If he'll be doing a lot of hiking, a large backpack is best. Be sure to select a frame pack that fits his body and feels comfortable fully loaded. (Almost any backpack feels comfy in the store when it's empty.) If your child will be doing only day-long hikes, it's best to pack everything in a trunk, but bring a separate day pack. If the living quarters are like a dorm room, with closets and drawers, then a duffel bag may be the best container. Once unpacked, duffel bags can be folded and stuffed under his bed or in a drawer. If the living quarters don't have drawers, trunks keep clothes and gear neater than suitcases, backpacks, and duffel bags.

Packing list tips

Now that you understand the five most important principles of packing for overnight camp, let's turn to a specific list of items. This isn't an actual packing list for a real camp; it's just a list of ideas about certain items that you may be packing. Remember, you need to refer to the camp's own clothing and equipment list to know exactly what and how much to bring. This annotated list is divided into seven parts: Headgear, Clothing,

Just for kids
Time-Tested Trunk Tips

- Choose a trunk that has a top tray. This provides a neat space for stationery, toiletries, and miscellaneous items.

- Get in the habit of closing the buckles on the front of the trunk. The traditional design has brass buckles that stick straight out when opened. Campers call these "shin busters" for good reasons!

- Most trunks come with simple locking latch and key. Because most camps don't allow campers to lock their trunks, you may want to remove the lock or place duct tape over it. If the lock is left in place, there's a good chance it will get shut with the key inside! If your camp allows trunks to be locked, store one key outside the trunk, and give the other key to your cabin leader.

- Put your name on the outside and inside of the trunk to identify it. You can also personalize your trunk with cool stickers and designs. Just make sure the content is appropriate for camp. If you're not sure about a sticker, don't put it on your trunk.

Footwear, Bedding and Towels, Toiletries, Other Gear, and Things Not to Bring. Items are alphabetized within each category.

Headgear

❏ **Bandanna/Headband/Scrunchie.** These keep hair and sweat out of your face during games, matches, climbs, sailing, cooking, and arts and crafts.

❏ **Hats.** Hats keep the sun out of your eyes during activities, protecting your skin from harmful ultraviolet (UV) rays. They also keep ticks off you during hikes. Baseball caps are the most popular. Beach hats are also fun. A wide-brimmed hat that shades the shoulders and upper back is best for kids who sunburn easily.

❏ **Prescription Lenses.** If you wear glasses or contacts, it's a good idea to bring an extra pair in case one gets lost or damaged. Leave the spare pair with the health center staff.

❏ **Sunglasses.** The best sunglasses block 95-100% of UV rays. Cheap pairs often provide little or no UV protection and can actually harm your eyes. Buy a strap, such as Croakies® or Cat Straps®, to keep them on, plus a solid case to protect them when you're not wearing them.

❏ **Swimming Goggles.** Use them during swim lessons, especially when you're trying new skills that involve putting your face in the water or actually swimming underwater. Goggles also reduce eye irritation from chlorinated pools and are a must for kids who want to be on the camp swim team.

Clothing

❏ **Bathrobe.** Some camps suggest a bathrobe; others don't. Typically, campers wear bathrobes to stay warm on the walk between the living quarters and the bathroom or shower center. Even if the camp doesn't suggest a bathrobe, you may feel more comfortable wearing one after a shower than wrapping yourself with a towel for the walk back to your cabin. Cotton terry cloth is best. Flannel is not bad, but not as absorbent. Silk is too formal and delicate for camp.

❏ **Dress Clothes.** Bring dress shirts and pants or skirts for religious services, dances, golf, and other dressy activities. Remember matching shoes and a belt.

❏ **Jacket/Windbreaker.** You'll need one for activities on cool or windy days, such as sailing or hiking. Something you can stuff in a compartment or day pack is perfect. Water-proof but breathable fabric, such as Gore-Tex®, is excellent. Although costly, many Gore-Tex® jackets double as raincoats, so they may be worth the investment. Jackets and vests made of Polartec® or generic polyester/rayon fleece are also great. This special fabric wicks away moisture, is non-allergenic and washable, insulates even when wet, and can easily be layered under a waterproof shell.

❑ **Jeans.** Jeans were invented for a reason. Levi Strauss had some miner friends who needed rugged pants. It's no surprise that such a good invention has withstood the test of time. There's no substitute for a good pair of jeans. For camp, avoid bringing acid-washed or distressed jeans. Worn denim might look nice, but the weakened fabric is prone to ripping. Get a rugged pair of jeans you can use for horseback riding, hiking in the woods, capture-the-flag, and just walking around.

❑ **Raincoat.** This is an item where quality really matters. Buy a coat that is truly waterproof, not just water-repellent. Cheap plastic ponchos are compact and may be useful in some cases, but they tear in heavy wind and snag on tree branches. Some cheap ponchos are basically just plastic bags with a hood. If you like the poncho style, buy something durable. Whatever you buy, make sure it has a waterproof hood. There's nothing as chilling as drizzle down the back of your neck.

❑ **Shorts.** Unless it's a winter camp, most kids wear shorts every day at overnight camp, so pack at least five pair. Although athletic shorts, such as nylon soccer shorts, are generally fine, shorts with pockets are best for hikes and field trips.

❑ **Sweatshirt/Sweater.** Bring at least one; two if the camp is in a cool climate. Cotton and most artificial fabrics lose their insulating power when wet, so wool or synthetic fleece is superior. Reverse-weave cotton sweatshirts are best for dry weather.

❑ **Swim Suits.** Choose a suit made of a fabric that dries quickly, such as nylon or lycra. Heavy cotton suits or shorts may take several days to dry. Putting on a cold, damp suit is pretty uncomfortable and can cause chafing and rashes. Boys should choose a suit with a liner and a drawstring waist to make sure the suit stays put. By the same token, most girls prefer one-piece suits at camp because they stay on better than bikinis. Kids interested in the camp swim team should pack a racing suit.

❑ **T-shirts/Tank Tops.** Campers live in their favorite T-shirts. Include one or two long-sleeve T-shirts for cool evenings or to wear under an itchy wool sweater. Don't pack shirts that might offend people, such as those with sexual humor, alcohol or tobacco advertisements, marijuana leaves, or profanity.

❑ **Underwear.** Although it may seem that seven pairs for seven days would be plenty, many campers end up swimming in shorts and underwear, thus relegating several pair to the clothes line. Also, there may be a day or two lag in laundry service. We recommend you use the formula in the previous section to calculate the number of pairs of underwear you should bring. Pack at least $1^1/_2$ times the number of days between laundry services.

❑ **Warm-Up Pants/Sweat Pants.** For evenings, cool days, and activities where you might slide on the ground, you'll want to bring warm-up pants or sweat pants. Nylon warm-up pants or wind pants are popular, but the flimsy ones tear easily. Pack a belt if the pants don't have a drawstring or elastic waist.

For Young Women:

❑ **Bras.** If the camp has an aquatics program, you'll probably spend half the day in your bathing suit. Still, if you normally wear a bra, you should pack the same number of bras as you do underwear. At camp, many young women prefer cotton sports bras because they're easier to play in. It's your choice. However, if you bring regular bras, you should also bring a small net bag to put them in for laundry service. Don't forget to label the bag.

For Young Men:

❑ **Athletic Supporters.** Young men may wish to bring jock straps for sports that involve running or jumping, such as basketball, soccer, tennis, or track. Horseback riding is also more comfortable when wearing an athletic supporter. Some young men prefer boxer-length briefs or compression shorts to athletic supporters. Those who play football, lacrosse, the catcher position in baseball, or the goalie position in hockey may wish to bring an athletic supporter with a protective cup.

Footwear

❑ **Boots.** You'll need boots for hikes, horseback riding, and muddy, rainy days. Like sneakers, make sure you have the right kind of boot for the activities that you plan to do at camp. If the boots are old, check the heels and soles. Repair them if necessary. If the boots are not waterproof, buy some waterproofing liquid, spray, or paste at your local supermarket, department store, pharmacy, or shoe store. Check the laces to be sure they will last.

❑ **Cleats.** Cleats are optional for some children, but necessary for those interested in playing soccer, baseball, football, field hockey, ultimate Frisbee, rugby, and other field sports. We recommend you waterproof your cleats, as you did with your boots. Even if your camp is in a dry climate, there might be enough morning dew on the fields to soak your cleats. If you have screw-in cleats, be sure there is no metal showing, and pack your cleat wrench. Soccer players should also pack shin guards and soccer socks.

❑ **Dress Shoes and Socks/Nylons.** If you're packing dress clothes, you'll need shoes and socks or sandals that match the outfit. Girls may wish to pack nylons or leggings.

❑ **Sandals/Flip-flops.** These are both useful and popular. However, sandals are not meant for hiking or sports, despite the advertisements. Hiking or playing sports in a pair of rubber or cork sandals can lead to crushed toes, broken toenails, and twisted ankles. Use sandals for walking around camp, which you'll do a lot. For sports, wear the appropriate sneakers, cleats, or boots.

❑ **Sneakers.** It's a good idea to have two pairs of sneakers: one newer pair for sports and one older pair for everyday wear. Make sure the laces on both pairs are new, so they will survive the summer. If you plan to play tennis, you must bring sneakers with white rubber soles that will not mar court surfaces. If you plan to play basketball, you should bring high-tops that provide proper ankle support.

❑ **Socks.** There are many theories to explain where all the missing

socks go. Perhaps they migrate south or hide in the dryer. Maybe they enter the fourth dimension. Whatever the reason, the number of socks you bring to camp will always be greater than or equal to the number of socks you bring home. Therefore, pack a lot of socks, and make sure that they are appropriate for the shoes you'll be wearing. Pack thick wool socks for your hiking boots, and all-white, crew-length, cotton-blend socks for sports.

Bedding and towels

From the camp information packet, you should learn what kind of bedding to bring. This can range from nothing at all (if the camp is

supplying all the sheets, blankets, and pillows) to everything (if the camp supplies only a cot, bed, platform, or bare earth).

❑ **Bedroll.** If the sleeping accommodations at camp do not include a mattress, bring a bedroll as a substitute. These light, inexpensive foam pads are available at department stores and camping outfitters. Kids' backs love the extra cushioning.

❑ **Blanket.** This can be a good substitute for a sleeping bag on warmer nights and a nice addition to a bag on cooler nights. Our favorite camp blankets are made of wool, Polartec® fleece, or a similar fabric. They retain their insulating qualities even when damp.

❑ **Mattress Pad.** Many camps use plastic mattress covers that can feel and sound a bit crunchy under a sheet or sleeping bag. A mattress pad will make your camp bunk more comfortable and homey.

❑ **Pillow & Pillow Cases.** These are easy to forget, but so important to remember. Your living quarters at camp will feel more like home if you're resting your head on your own pillow. Even if the camp supplies pillows, you still may want to bring your own. Remember to pack at least two pillow cases so you can use one while the other is in the laundry.

❑ **Sheets.** Sheets are a must, so bring one if the camp doesn't provide them. On sweltering summer nights, there's nothing quite as comfy and refreshing as a flat cotton sheet. Sleeping bags can turn into saunas. If the camp supplies mattresses, pack a fitted sheet in addition to a flat sheet. Even if your camp says that all you need is a sleeping bag, a soft fitted sheet can make a plastic mattress cover much more comfortable. Many camp mattresses are an obscure extra-long twin size (39"x80") or a narrow cot size. If you cannot find the correct size fitted sheet, or if you don't want to spend extra money, a regular twin-size flat sheet will work fine with some creative tucking and a few safety pins.

❏ **Sleeping Bag.** There are two factors to consider for sleeping bags: size and warmth. As for size, you want a bag that fits you comfortably. As for warmth, you must consider the conditions in which you'll be camping. Most quality bags have a warmth rating, such as 20°F or -10°F, that indicates their insulation power. For typical summer overnight camps, you won't need a bag rated to arctic temperatures. In fact, that could be really uncomfortable in hot, humid weather. If you plan to backpack or camp outdoors, get a bag recommendation from the camp.

❏ **Hand Towels.** These are the best thing to use for washing up because they dry faster than a beach or bath towel. Two or three hand towels should be plenty.

❏ **Large Towels.** Large beach or bath towels are treated cruelly and left all around camp, so find some older ones around your house, and pack three or four. Cotton terrycloth is best.

Toiletries

❏ **Toiletry or Dop Kit.** These kits are handy because you may have to walk from your living quarters to the bathrooms and showers. Choose a plastic, vinyl, or fabric kit, as opposed to leather, which rots if it stays wet. Here's what kids should include in their kit:

❏ **Baby Powder or Foot Powder.** This is excellent for counteracting strong odors and preventing chafing in hot weather.

❏ **Comb or Brush.** There's no need to bring blow dryers or curling irons. This is camp, not school.

❑ **Deodorant/Anti-Perspirant.** If you use deodorant, remember that most camps do not allow aerosols, so pack a stick or roll-on.

❑ **Feminine Hygiene Products.** Female campers who have not yet menstruated should still bring pads or tampons in case they have their first period at camp.

❑ **Insect Repellent.** As with deodorant, don't pack an aerosol can. Get lotion or stick repellent instead. Try some at home to be sure you're not allergic to it. Don't use 100% deet (N,N-diethyl-meta-toluamide) repellents unless your camp is located deep in the boggy woods. Deet repellent is powerful but hazardous if used incorrectly. Something milder, such as OFF® lotion or Cutter's® stick repellent will probably suffice.

❑ **Lip Balm.** Sun, cold, and dry weather can all chap lips, especially if you're not used to those environments.

❑ **Nail Clippers.** Bring these for any camp stay longer than a week.

❑ **Shampoo.** The kind with conditioner saves space.

❑ **Shaving Gear.** (If you need it.)

❑ **Soap & Soap Box.** Make sure the soap box closes securely. If you normally use special soap for acne or sensitive skin, be sure to bring that, along with any skin creams or lotions you use.

❑ **Sunblock.** Choose SPF 15 or higher; waterproof if possible. Use it often.

❑ **Tissues.** These are always handy, and more sanitary than a shirt sleeve.

❑ **Toothbrush & Holder.** The holder will keep the brush from getting dirty.

❑ **Toothpaste.** Get a regular-size tube, not a dinky travel tube.

Other Gear

❑ **Bean Bag Ball.** Bean bag balls or Hackey Sacks® are a popular and fun way to improve coordination for field sports like soccer. You might not like bean bags at all, but we put this on the list as an example of the best kind of toy you can bring to camp. It's fun, small, inexpensive, rugged, doesn't need batteries, and can be

played with a group of friends. If you can, bring a few toys with
these specifications to camp.

❑ **Books/Magazines.** All overnight camps have some quiet time
built into their schedule. Good books and magazines fill this time
well. Summer reading lists from
schools are excellent choices, but
make sure you pack a few other
selections as well.

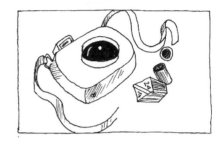

❑ **Camera.** Disposable cameras are
best. They are sturdy, take decent
pictures, and if they get lost or
broken, it's no big deal.
Environmentally conscious families can purchase recycled
disposable cameras at natural foods stores.

❑ **Fishing Pole & Tackle Box.** Some camps near water have
excellent fishing. Just be sure to leave any knives at home.
Knives aren't allowed at most camps. Instead of a fillet knife,
pack a small pair of manicure scissors for snipping line, and let
the camp chef fillet your catch.

❑ **Flashlight.** Pack a durable, bright flashlight. Pack extra
alkaline batteries and a spare bulb. Don't rely on those little key
chains that light up when you squeeze them. They're cute, but
they don't last long. They may be perfect for lighting your
keyhole, but useless in the dark woods.

❑ **Flying Disk.** Frisbees®, Aerobies®, and other flying disks are
like bean bag balls—fun, small, inexpensive, almost unbreakable,
without batteries, and playable with a group of friends. A flying
disk is an ideal toy to bring to camp. Remember to label it with a
laundry marker.

❑ **Glasses Repair Kit.** Some camps are far from glasses repair
shops, so if you wear glasses, you may want to pack a small
screwdriver and extra screws for loose bows or nosepieces. These
kits are inexpensive and available at most drug stores. You might
also pack some lens cleaning cloths.

❑ **Laundry Bag.** Not all camps require campers to have individual
laundry bags, but it helps. Buy one that's big enough to hold a

week's worth of clothes, with a draw-string closure to prevent odors from escaping. Remember to label it, just like everything else. If possible, wash the bag with the rest of your clothes on laundry day.

❏ **Musical Instruments.** Although many musical instruments are delicate, music and camp go together, and having an instrument at camp is a great way to make new friends. Guitars, brass instruments, woodwinds, and harmonicas are especially popular. If you are uncertain about whether your instrument will have a safe home at camp, call the camp and ask. Also, check with the camp before bringing large instruments or electric instruments and amplifiers. Campers may not have access to electrical outlets, and amplified music may be against the camp's policy.

❏ **Personal Stereos and Headphones.** If personal stereos are allowed by the camp, you may wish to bring one. Music is a good diversion during quiet times at camp. However, like everything else you bring to camp, there's a chance it will get broken. Don't bring anything that would be difficult to replace. Remember to pack extra alkaline batteries, and respect your fellow campers by not blasting your personal stereo.

❏ **Playing Cards.** A deck of playing cards or a card game such as Uno® is perfect for camp.

❏ **Sock Bag.** This handy invention is designed to hold all your dirty socks. When you throw the full bag in the laundry, the socks get washed, but stay in the bag. This makes for effortless sorting when the laundry comes back. One good brand is the Sockmonster Sak™. You can also purchase a zippered mesh bag at any discount department store or outdoor supply store.

❏ **Sports/Specialty Equipment.** Good camps should be fully stocked with all the equipment that a camper needs to participate in daily activities. However, many kids enjoy bringing their own equipment, especially if it's broken-in and they're used to using it. You may want to bring your tennis racquet, lacrosse stick, baseball glove, rock-climbing shoes, or soccer shin guards. If you're attending a specialty overnight camp, check the information packet to see whether you need to bring certain equipment or supplies, such as riding boots, computer disks, tennis balls, or a helmet.

Just for kids
Pack Like a Pro

- Label everything. We can't say this enough, so we'll keep on saying it. Label everything.
- Make a list of everything that you're bringing to camp and tape it to the inside of your trunk or suitcase. If you're packing into a backpack or duffel bag, put that list in one of the pockets. Use the list at the end of camp to make sure you haven't forgotten anything!
- Instead of stacking folded clothes in your trunk or suitcase, roll the clothes neatly and pack them upright like pencils in a jar. That way, you can see everything that you have, without unpacking a thing!
- Pack small items in zippered plastic bags so they all stay put.

❑ **Water Bottle or Canteen.** The best ones are made of tough plastic or metal and seal completely when you screw the top on. You don't want water leaking all over your backpack or sleeping bag. Big plastic cups with built-in straws are OK for working out or playing tennis, but you can't take them on hiking trips because they leak and spill.

❑ **Writing Paper/Envelopes/Stamps.** Humidity is the enemy of envelopes and stamps. If you're not careful, everything will stick together and become useless. There are two ways to combat this problem. Either seal your envelopes and stamps in a big zippered plastic freezer bag, or buy "no-lick" self-sealing envelopes and adhesive stamps. Pack all the stationery, envelopes, and stamps you will need. Many camps do not sell stationery or stamps.

To ensure some correspondence from camp, many parents buy pre-stamped postcards or envelopes at the post office and address them ahead of time to home, grandparents, and important friends. Many families use computer labels and printers to pre-address entire batches of envelopes. If you don't pre-address envelopes, be sure you pack the addresses of family and friends. Kids should know how to properly address an envelope. Every summer we see postcards addressed simply to "Mom and Dad."

Things NOT to Bring

- **Electronics.** Many camps ban electronic equipment, including personal stereos, handheld video games, portable stereos, laptops, palmtops, televisions, beepers, and cellular phones. If you want to bring electronics to camp, check the information packet first, to be sure it's allowed. Even if electronics are allowed, consider leaving them at home and enjoying nature, a book, outdoor activities, or your cabin mates' company instead.

- **Food.** We advise against bringing food and storing it in your cabin, unless that's the usual practice at your camp. On the one hand, food in the cabin is like a giant neon "Welcome!" sign for ants, mice, and other critters. Food in the cabin also discourages campers from eating the balanced meals that the camp chef prepares for them. On the other hand, junk food and home-baked goodies are fun treats. Find out what is allowed at your camp, and plan accordingly. All campers should remember to share the food they bring and receive.

- **Over the Counter (OTC) Drugs.** Drugs available without a prescription, such as cough syrup, aspirin, and other pain relievers, are still drugs, and drugs are not allowed at most camps. Don't worry, the camp health center or infirmary will have everything you need if you are injured or sick. Many parents think they can send OTC drugs with their children because they know their children are responsible, but that's not the issue. Other kids might go through your stuff and use those drugs in an irresponsible way. Certain OTC drugs can be dangerous to campers who do not know how to use them. That's why, at most camps, campers are only allowed to keep asthma inhalers and bug repellent with them. If you think your medical situation necessitates your carrying OTC drugs around camp, discuss it with the camp director in the months before camp starts. Chances are, you'll be able to find a workable solution. Some camps do allow kids to keep certain OTC drugs.

– **Tobacco/Alcohol/Illegal Drugs.** Camp is a place to be naturally high. Most camps will immediately send kids home for use or possession of tobacco, alcohol, illegal drugs or drug paraphernalia.

– **Weapons/Flammables/Explosives.** This is overnight camp, not Army boot camp. Knives, guns, matches, lighters, brass knuckles, box cutters, fireworks, and any other weapons are strictly forbidden. If your fishing tackle box includes a knife, you should leave it at home. If you'd like to bring a pocket knife for camping, find out whether that's permitted.

Now you and your child can return to the packing list provided by your camp. Start assembling all the items that she's bringing to camp, and check them off the list as you go.

Checklist

- ❑ Label everything.
- ❑ Wash and wear before camp.
- ❑ Prepare for losses.
- ❑ Consider laundry frequency.
- ❑ Pack in the recommended container.

PART IV

GETTING THE MOST OUT OF CAMP

CHAPTER 12

Opening day

When I was a camper, I counted the days until camp opened. When opening day finally dawned, I was excited but nervous; eager but wary. Camp meant fun and seeing old friends, but it also meant new friends and new experiences, and thus a bit of uncertainty. Even to this day, a wave of anxious excitement comes over me as I cover the last few miles to the familiar sign that welcomes me home to camp.

—Hank, age 23, 7th year cabin leader

Opening day is exciting, but also a bit chaotic . . . for everyone. Campers are anxious to learn about their cabin assignment, meet their cabin leader and fellow campers, and perform well on the swim check. Parents are nervous about leaving their child in someone else's care, wondering whether their child will love camp as much as they did, and uncertain what the next few weeks will be like without their son or daughter at home. Cabin leaders are tense about meeting parents, remembering their former campers' names, and being judged by new campers. The rest of the staff is worried about parking, registration, and suddenly having to feed all the new campers. Directors are charged up about everything. They have worked for ten months to prepare for this single, spectacular day.

Parents and kids enjoy the magic of opening day when they are organized and prepared—both mentally and physically. Here's how, in six simple steps.

1. Make a travel plan.

Some families will be driving directly from home, or from a relative's house, to camp. Others will be driving their child to a bus terminal, airport, or train station. Whatever your child's exact route to camp, estimate first how much time you need to drive to camp, or to the bus, plane, or train. Then, add an hour or two. This will allow time to stop and buy a pillow, toothpaste, or whatever you or your child suddenly remember you forgot. Use any leftover time to visit with one another before you say good-bye.

Plan the trip to be relaxing, regardless of your mode of transportation. If camp opens in the afternoon, plan a stop for lunch. Remember, though, that if the camp is in a small town, roads and restaurants may be congested with your child's future cabin mates. If registration begins early in the morning, and camp is far from home, it's sometimes easier to stay overnight near the camp. A little planning now will minimize problems later. Being hungry, late, or sleepy can quickly turn the excitement of opening day into stress. This is a happy day, so make a plan that allows for a snag or two. If problems do arise, don't panic.

2. Complete registration.

Honor the time that your camp sets for registration. Most camps do the bulk of their setup in the week before camp opens. In fact, there is work to do right up until the hour before registration. Arriving extra early can interfere with last-minute staff preparations.

Registration is a way for the camp to ensure that everyone who is scheduled to arrive actually makes it. The process generally involves meeting the directors, checking in to settle your child's account, getting a cabin assignment, talking to the medical staff if necessary, moving your child's gear to her cabin, and meeting her new cabin leader.

Parents who are not coming to camp with their children must correspond with the camp before opening day. You'll need to accomplish all the things on the end of the chapter Checklist by phone or mail.

3. Meet your child's cabin leader.

Your child's cabin, bunk, tent, or unit may have more than one leader, but make sure you meet at least one of them. Ask about their camping experience, where they are in school, how their summer has been going, and where they live. You should leave camp with a good sense of who is caring for your child. Communicate any physical, behavioral, or

Just for kids
Too many names?
Make a crazy sentence to remember!

You're going to meet a lot of new people at camp. How will you remember all their names?

Here's a trick for remembering your cabin mates' names: Make a crazy sentence that tells you the first letter of each kid's name.

First, write down everyone's name on a piece of paper. Or, look at a cabin list, if there's already one printed. Then, underline the first letter of each name. For example, if there are five other campers in your cabin, they might be named Pat, Robin, Chris, Francis and Bo. Then, you take the letters P, R, C, F, and B and try to make a crazy sentence out of them.

Your crazy sentence might be, "Pink Rabbits Can Fly Busses." Then, if you can't remember someone's name, just say to yourself, "Pink rabbits can fly busses," and you should remember the first letter of the name you're searching for. Knowing that beginning letter will help you remember the whole name.

You can also ask your cabin leader to play the "Name Game." One person starts by trying to name everyone else in the cabin. When he's thought of all the names he can, the next person tries, and so on. This is a good way for everyone to practice other kids' names.

emotional concerns you have about your child, and tell the cabin leader how you usually deal with these issues. If your child takes medications or has any allergies, share this information too. Remember, the more the leader understands about your child from the start, the better time they will both have.

Also, talk with the cabin leader about your child's previous experience away from home and current feelings about coming to camp. Leaders like to know which campers might struggle with the separation, and which veteran campers they can count on to help orient the rookies. If applicable, you may want to mention exceptional family circumstances, such as a recent divorce, loss of a loved one or pet, or a traumatic academic, social, or athletic event. Personal details aren't necessary, but a basic understanding of what has been happening in your child's life can put his emotions and behaviors in perspective for the camp staff. When we were cabin leaders, such information helped us steer around sensitive topics during spontaneous night-time discussions with our cabins. Of course, sharing family history is up to you and your child. Many parents choose to include their child in these conversations with cabin leaders. Emphasize to your child's cabin leader the importance of confidentiality, if you judge it's appropriate.

Cabin Leaders' Views of Opening Day

"My best opening day memories are of parents who greeted me as if I were a long lost son. They bounded out of the family car smiling, often more excited than their child. Some even brought food (which was allowed on change days) or a more valuable commodity—a newspaper. All this was much appreciated in the somewhat isolated world of overnight camp."

"My worst opening day memories are standing in a downpour for six hours greeting car after car after car."

"I once had a parent who just pulled up in front of my cabin and let his son out the passenger-side door. Didn't help with the bags, didn't greet me, and hardly said a word to his kid. Incredible and pretty rough for a kid."

"I really like it when parents ask me questions. I spend so much time asking them questions about their kid, it's nice when they take an interest in me. After all, I'm like a substitute parent. They should care."

While talking with your child's cabin leader, respect his or her responsibilities to other parents. It's not uncommon for several families to arrive at one cabin simultaneously. Everyone is unpacking their gear, two family dogs are running through the cabin, and a three-year-old baby brother is crying. This is a hectic scenario for a cabin leader who needs to spend time with each set of parents. You may have to wait your turn to have a decent talk, but it's worth your while.

If you cannot be there in person on opening day, you should still share as much helpful information as you can with your child's cabin leader. The best way to do this is by writing a descriptive letter to the camp director. The director can pass it on to your child's cabin leader when cabin assignments are made. As cabin leaders, we loved to get these letters, because they helped us get to know the children with whom we'd be working. Before they ever set foot in our cabins, we knew their likes and dislikes, and how to relate to them as individuals.

4. Address medical, behavioral, and emotional concerns.

If your child has any medical, behavioral, or emotional concerns, you should talk with the camp director and a representative of the medical staff. You can do this in person during registration, or by phone a few days before opening day. Both the camp director and the camp nurse or doctor should know about any medical conditions (asthma, allergies, recent injuries and illnesses, physical disabilities, etc.) and emotional or behavioral concerns (ADHD, eating disorders, bedwetting, sleepwalking, Tourette's syndrome, recent stressful family events, etc.) that your child has. At the very least, medical staff need to know about any medications your child is currently on, or has recently stopped taking. Find out who will administer the medication and how they will ensure adherence. Be sure to send any prescription medications in their original bottles with dosage instructions. Remember, the camp staff is there to help.

Some parents and children hesitate to share information about medical, emotional, or behavioral concerns. They may feel that the information is too personal, or they worry about confidentiality. If you want certain information to be confidential, simply tell the camp director. It's the director's ethical obligation to honor your request if it's in the best interest of your child. Other families hesitate to share information because they think the problem won't exist if no one knows about it. Often, this is a false hope. Staff usually notice that something is amiss, but they can't tell exactly what. They spend the entire session trying to define and assist with a problem that took time and money for parents and trained professionals to explain or diagnose. Had staff been informed about the problem up front, they could have helped out right away. The decision about whether to share information is up to you, of course. However, it is hardly ever beneficial to leave the camp in the dark about significant issues.

Finally, if you have packed over-the-counter medications in your child's trunk, check that the camp allows this. As we mentioned earlier, seemingly harmless medications, such as aspirin, can be dangerous in large doses. Sugar-based preparations, such as cough drops, attract ants and other animals and may be mistaken for candy by other kids. Camps prohibit children from keeping most medications in their cabin.

If your child has no medical, behavioral, or emotional issues, you might still want to say hello to the health center staff. They are the people who will care for your son or daughter in the unlikely event of an emergency.

5. Allocate spending money.

Most camps do not allow campers to keep cash with them. Therefore, the camp may ask you to allocate spending money for your child to purchase items at the camp store, buy projects at the arts and crafts shop, pay for out-of-camp trips, and so on. Some camps include spending money in the registration fees; others ask you to make a deposit when you register. If the camp does not publish a suggested amount in their information packet, ask the director how much spending money is adequate. You'll get back whatever is leftover at the end of the session.

After registration, decide as a family how to spend this money. If the camp has a store that sells camp merchandise, consider buying these items together on opening day. Having some camp clothing or other paraphernalia can help increase a new camper's sense of belonging. Bring a laundry marker to label anything you buy. Three hundred identical camp T-shirts have a way of getting lost more quickly than socks!

6. Say good-bye.

As with the rest of opening day, the rule of thumb here is to plan, but remain flexible. Parents and kids should decide together how long they want to hang out with each other at camp before parents head home. Many campers want parents to leave as soon as they have moved into their cabin. "OK, Mom, you can go now!" isn't easy for a mother to hear, but it expresses a clear preference. Other children want their parents to stay longer. Here is where practice time away from home, such as a sleep-over, can bring valuable experience to bear. Having separated before, families know what their good-bye styles are. They know how to compromise to respect each others' preferences. How will you say good-bye? A short walk? A hug and a kiss? Just a hug? A high-five? Talking it over now will make your good-bye go more smoothly.

Once you've said good-bye, you should make a decisive departure. Lingering or returning unexpectedly after a short time can make your child increasingly anxious about when you might actually leave, because the plan you made before is apparently no longer in effect. Plus, when parents linger, other kids can become jealous or uncomfortable. They might also think that a child with lingering parents is needy, and therefore difficult to befriend.

You might see some unexpected separation behavior in your child. Every cabin leader has seen campers break down and cry when their

parents get ready to leave. Most have also seen campers struggle to rush their parents out of camp. Remember, you are sending your child to camp to gain independence. It may start right away, or it might not. If you sense that your child wants you to stay longer than you had anticipated, that's fine, but try to stick to your initial plan for saying good-bye. Acknowledge the feeling and then give your child a choice. You might say, "I can tell you'd like me to stay a while longer. It's hard to say good-bye. But we agreed that once we'd registered and you'd unpacked, I'd be on my way. We could say good-bye now or in ten minutes. Which time sounds better to you?"

Thinking ahead to visiting day and the end of camp

Camp has not even started, but you need to think about the next important day. This may either be a visiting day or the end of camp. If you know when the camp allows parents to pick up their kids, you can set a reunion time together now. Remember that predictability can decrease anxiety, but you can't be exact. It's best to decide on a pick-up time window, such as "between 9:00 a.m. and 10:00 a.m.," to allow for the

Camp Directors' Views of Opening Day

"The feeling I get when parents tell me how beautiful camp is, or how much their child gained from the experience is what I live and work for."

"Being asked to make last-minute changes in cabin or unit assignments is extremely difficult. I'd much rather parents discuss their preferences with me in the spring than on opening day."

"It's incredibly busy, but I like to meet each parent. I want to make sure that I answer their questions."

"I like the visibility I have on opening day. It's important to me that the parents see who's running the show, and that I am running it well."

inevitable traffic, detours, and other snags parents encounter on visiting days or closing days.

If the camp does have a visiting day, make every effort to come. A child whose parents couldn't find the time to visit feels hurt watching other kids' parents shower affection. If huge distances or emergency commitments make it impossible for you to come on visiting day, try to work out another arrangement. Although it's not as fun as seeing one's own parents, kids do enjoy going out with their friends and their friends' family on visiting day. To set up this kind of arrangement, you must call, write, or fax the camp and give permission to have your child taken out of camp by someone else. If possible, try to set up these arrangements weeks or months ahead of time. This will give your child time to adjust to the idea.

Some camps hand out fliers on opening day to remind parents when the closing date and time is. That's a great idea. If the camp doesn't provide a written reminder, parents should write their own reminder. One of most pitiful things that we witnessed as cabin leaders was a kid waiting for his parents to arrive on closing day, nearly three hours after the pick-up time had elapsed. We still remember the dreary look on his face when he explained, "My parents said they would be here by 2:00 and it's already 4:45." Scenarios like this one happen every summer. Of course, you're only human, but do your best to be on time.

Checklist

At Home:

- ❏ Make a travel plan
- ❏ Make a good-bye plan
- ❏ Recheck packing list
- ❏ Bring directions to camp
- ❏ Bring medical forms and any other camp paperwork
- ❏ Bring your son or daughter

At Camp:*

- ❏ Register/check-in
- ❏ Meet camp director
- ❏ Allocate spending money
- ❏ Talk to medical staff (if necessary)
- ❏ Meet child's cabin leader
- ❏ Ask about visiting policy
- ❏ Verify closing-day pick-up time
- ❏ Write down:
    1. the pick-up date and time
    2. your child's cabin name and number
    3. the cabin leader's name
    4. the exact mailing address of camp

* Parents who won't be with their child on opening day should complete this part of the checklist from home. Be sure your child knows where her registration paperwork is, who is picking her up, where her trunk key is, and other helpful travel details.

CHAPTER 13

Staying in touch

I remember, as a first-year camper, being so eager to get mail that I got caught up in an age-old practical joke. On Sunday, one of the cabin leaders would say, "We need some of you to run up to the baseball field and meet the mail helicopter." A bunch of us Cadets would start sprinting up to the field, until someone realized that mail doesn't come on Sundays. It was great to be eight.

—Hans, age 19

Getting a letter at camp was like winning the lottery.

When we were campers, our cabin leaders would walk in each afternoon holding a small stack of letters. They'd tease us a little by reading the return addresses. "Let see . . . does anyone know someone who lives at 32 Otsego Road?" One of us would recognize his home address and scream, "I do! I do! That's my dad! That one's for me!" We loved that game. We loved everything about getting mail. Sending it was another story.

In this chapter, we'll discuss the four basic ways you can keep in touch to help your child enjoy camp even more: letters, electronic messages (faxes and e-mails), phone calls, and care packages. At the end of the chapter, we'll give you some tips on enjoying visiting day, if your child's camp has one.

Letters

No news is good news when it comes to kids at camp. If you don't receive any letters from your child while she's at camp, you're not alone. The best you can do is pack pre-stamped, pre-addressed envelopes and paper, and write letters that encourage your child to write back. Every single letter you write will be deeply appreciated, but you may not get a reply. Generally, this means your child is having so much fun, there's no time to write. If you don't pack pre-stamped, pre-addressed envelopes for your child, be sure she knows how to address, return address, and stamp an envelope properly. Many kids don't, and their letters don't go far.

How do I write a good letter from home?

A good letter from home is newsy, upbeat, and encouraging. Your goal is to say a cheerful hello and give a positive report about what's been going on. You want to instill confidence and support your child's growing independence. Avoid mentioning sad things that your child can't do anything about. Save bad news until you can talk to your child face to face. Obviously, if there is a major piece of bad news to report, and you need to tell your son or daughter immediately, you wouldn't put that in a letter either. Instead, you'd call camp and talk to the director first. In a quality letter, it's fine to say that you miss your child, but don't say that you're miserable. Hearing bad news they can't do anything about makes kids feel helpless. Helplessness leads to homesickness, depression, and anxiety.

Here's an example of a good letter from home:

Dear Chris,

How is camp going? Did you get a chance to do archery yet? I know you were pretty excited about that when we dropped you off. I'm sure you're getting to try lots of fun new activities.

What's your cabin leader like? He sure seemed nice when I talked with him. I think that's pretty neat that he's going to the same college Aunt Kathy went to. What a coincidence!

Yesterday, I worked until about 4:30pm and then came home to weed the garden. I was surprised to find four big tomatoes that were already ripe! I picked them and brought them inside for dad to make spaghetti sauce later this week.

Spot is doing great. Dad and I take turns walking him. Yesterday, he found a tennis ball under the Borozan's hedges and he was running around trying to get me to play catch. I did for a while, but then the ball got really slimy. Yuck!

Dad has been working hard, and he's looking forward to this weekend. On Sunday, he'll probably watch the game and then we're cooking dinner for the Rutars. Do you remember Mr. and Mrs. Rutar? Mrs. Rutar was Danilo's math teacher in fourth grade. I haven't seen her since April.

I'm so happy that you had the chance to go to camp this summer, Chris. What a wonderful experience! I just loved camp when I was your age. My favorite part was singing songs. Have you learned any camp songs? What about camp cheers?

Dad and I miss you and we love you a lot. We'll be there to pick you up on Saturday the 16th. Until then, have a great time. I'll write more soon.

love, Mom

P.S. I cut out the last three Beekota cartoons from the paper and enclosed them. I'll send the Sunday cartoons on Monday. Enjoy!

This letter sounds a little contrived because it is. You can surely write something more personal and sincere. The strength of this sample is that it contains the key elements of a good letter from home: It's newsy, upbeat, and encouraging. Plus, it mentions when the parent will write again, and it contains a lot of questions. This invites the child to write back. (You can at least hope, right?) Finally, the letter includes some newspaper comics. Interesting, age-appropriate newspaper or magazine clippings add interest to your letters. You can also insert photographs or drawings or whatever you dream up that fits in an envelope.

Now compare that sample good letter to this pretend bad letter:

Dear Chris,

Do you miss me? I sure do miss you. Sometimes, I just sit around and think about what we'd be doing if you were here. Even Spot misses you. When I take him for a walk, he doesn't seem as peppy as he usually does. Maybe he's sick.

I'm really sorry to tell you that one of your hamsters died. I've been feeding them every day, so I don't know what happened. At least there's one left. He seems lonely.

Not much else is new around here. It's actually pretty boring. Dad and I have both been working. Yesterday I weeded the garden. You know: same old, same old. The tomatoes are ripe now, so they'll probably be gone by the time you get home.

Speaking of home, I hope you're not homesick. You're too old for that. Plus, camp is a luxury, you know. A lot of kids never get to go to a camp like yours.

Don't forget to eat your vegetables. How is the food, by the way? I remember when I went to camp, years ago, the food was awful. The worst was "Mystery Meat." I never did figure out what they put in there. Yuck! Well, see you soon.

love, Mom

You'd think that no one would ever write a letter this awful, but campers have shown us a few that came close. Parents don't write this kind of dreary letter on purpose, it just comes out. They don't think about the effect it will have.

The sample above contains all sorts of elements of a poor letter from home. It dwells on how much the parent misses the child and it provides several pieces of bad news. It almost guarantees to make the child homesick by giving him lots to worry about. Is my dog sick? How is my other hamster doing? Will there be any tomatoes left? Are my parents doing OK, or are they bored to death? What's in my food? When will Mom send the next letter? This sample bad letter also gives the child things to feel guilty about. Was the hamster's death my fault? If I don't like camp, am I a bad person? Mom says I'm "too old" for homesickness, but I feel it anyway. Am I normal? Will she be mad if I tell her?

We hope you laughed a little at how bad that sample bad letter was. Now you won't worry about writing something that might make your child uncomfortable or homesick. But what if she is homesick? Every parent dreads receiving the classic Homesick-at-Camp letter. How do you respond? Let's take a look at some sample homesick letters.

Dear Mom and Dad,
Camp is terribal. I am homesick almost every minnut. I tried evrything, and nothing works. I need to come home rite now! Please, please, please come and get me today!

love, Ruthie

Or what about this one . . .

Dear Mom and Dad,
This camp stinks! The counsillers are all mean and so are the kids. All I want to do is come home. If you dont come pick me up, I am going to run away. I swayr. I hate this place!

your son, Brandon

How can parents respond to letters like these? Most parents have one, natural, first instinct: Get in the car and go get the kid. Then they realize that would defeat the purpose of the whole overnight camping experience. A shortened stay should be a last resort, not a first one. We'll discuss shortened stays later (see page 211). For now, let's stick with writing good letters.

The second instinct that most parents have is to call the camp. That's a better instinct, but remember, you should be calling to talk with the camp director or to your child's cabin leader, not to your child.

What about calling the camp regarding my child's homesickness?

When you get a letter like the samples above, it's appropriate to call the camp and talk to a staff member who can give you a status report. Most times, that person will tell you that your child has gotten over her homesickness and is doing fine. Surprised? You shouldn't be. Remember two things. First, the letter you got is several days old. A lot can happen at camp in three or four days. Second, the letter was obviously written during a moment of desperation. Things may have changed immediately after the letter was mailed.

If you do call, what should you ask? First, identify yourself as a parent of a current camper, and state why you're calling. Then ask to talk with your child's cabin leader. Talking to the cook or the nurse or whoever else happens to be answering the phone that day won't do any good. You need to talk with someone who is in frequent contact with your child. After you've made your request clear, be prepared to wait on the line a while, or to hang up and wait for a call back. Most overnight camps are large, dispersed campuses with few phones. Your child's cabin leader may be running an activity far from a phone when you call. Perhaps your message won't even get to him until the next mealtime, when he's closer to a phone.

When you eventually do get to talk to your child's cabin leader, tell him about the letter. Don't be surprised if the cabin leader never detected any homesickness. Research has demonstrated that many severely homesick campers go unnoticed by their cabin leaders. It's not that the cabin leaders don't care, or that they don't know what to look for. Sometimes, it's simply that children hide their feelings from grown-ups they don't know well.

Once your child's cabin leader understands your concern, he can tell you how your child is currently doing. Chances are, he's doing much better. However, if he's still homesick, you'll want to hear what the cabin leader's plans are for helping the situation. Feel free to make suggestions for this plan. After all, you know your child better than anyone.

If your child's letter contained a threat to run away (or to do anything else unsafe), be sure to discuss that with both the cabin leader and the camp director. No one is in a position to call your child's bluff. It's not safe to assume that his threat to run away was an empty threat. You have to take it seriously. If your child isn't homesick anymore, running away isn't an issue. However, if he's still severely homesick, someone at camp needs to "contract for safety" with your child. It's rare that cabin leaders need to contract for safety with campers, but it's worth mentioning so you understand the concept.

Contracting for safety means that the cabin leader or the camp director will sit down with your child and say something like, "Brandon, your mom called on the phone today because she got a letter from you that made her worried. Do you remember what you wrote that might have made her worried? That's right, it was the part about running away. Now, I know you've been feeling really homesick lately, and we've been working on that. But running away is a really unsafe way to deal with your homesick feelings. I don't think it will solve the problem, and you might get hurt. So you and I need to have an agreement. If you ever feel like you're really going to run away, do you agree to come and talk with me first? That way, we can find a safer way to help you feel better. Can you agree to that plan?"

If your child can agree to this sort of verbal safety contract, then he can stay at camp and keep working with the cabin leader on coping with his homesickness. However, if he refuses to contract for safety and continues to threaten to run away, then he needs constant staff supervision and a new plan of action. Children who cannot contract for safety are good candidates for shortened stays. Most camp staffs are not equipped to offer children prolonged, continuous, one-to-one supervision. If your child cannot contract for safety, then it's time to have a discussion with the camp director about your child's short-term supervision at camp and his immediate return home.

This may all sound a bit severe, but don't be concerned. Cases like this are extremely rare. It's just nice to know what you would do in an exceptional circumstance. Let's get back to discussing the much more common case of a child who's homesick, but not threatening to do something unsafe.

Before you hang up the phone, set up a specific day and time when your child's cabin leader will call you back. It will be important to check back in a day or so to see whether the plan for helping your child's homesickness is working. Remind the cabin leader by saying something like, "OK, then, you'll call me on Tuesday afternoon around 3:00 p.m. and give me an update? Thanks."

How do I write back to my child about homesickness?

Whether you decide to call camp or not, you should promptly write a letter back to your child about her homesickness. However, it's not easy to write these sorts of letters. Just like every other letter you write to your child at camp, you want this one to be newsy, upbeat, and encouraging. To this recipe, you must now add empathetic statements—words that show you understand how she feels. Once your child knows that you truly understand how upset she feels, she'll start to feel better.

Here's a sample response to the homesick letter on page 176.

Dear Ruthie,

I got your letter today about how homesick you've been feeling. I could tell, just by reading the letter, how much those homesick feelings bother you. I remember we talked about homesick feelings being normal, but I guess we didn't expect them to be so strong. It took a lot of courage to write that letter and tell me how bad you've been feeling. Thanks for letting me know.

Remember when we decided together that you wanted to go to camp? One of the things we talked about was how long you were going to stay, and we agreed on two weeks. That must seem like a really long time right now. But, by the time you get this letter, there will only be one week left of camp. Imagine, you've made it half way! That's a lot. You must be proud to have made it that far.

Maybe you're not so homesick anymore. I won't know for sure until I get your next letter. If you still are, remember all the things you can think and do to help make things better. Stay busy, write a lot of letters, talk to your cabin leader, and look on the bright side. There are lots of fun things to do at camp that you can't do at home. And before you know it, you'll be home. Seven more days is not that much. I know you can do it!

Rover says "hi." When you come home next week, we can take him out for a long walk in the park. He'll like that. The park has a baseball diamond, too, so you can show me how good your batting has gotten since you've been at camp.

Daddy and I miss you and love you. We'll be there to pick you up on Saturday morning, at the end of the session, just like we planned. Write again soon, sweetheart.

love, Mom

P.S. Here are some pictures from last weekend. Daddy and I went up to Yilfer to visit his old friend Tommy G. Pretty flowers, huh?

This letter is a healthy response because Mom stays positive and makes Ruthie feel understood. She normalizes homesickness, but acknowledges that Ruthie's feelings are unexpectedly strong. Mom also encourages Ruthie and reminds her that they decided together how long she would be at camp. More importantly, Mom helps Ruthie cope with her homesick feelings by reframing time and reminding her of the things that worked best during practice separations before camp started. For now, Mom is also sticking to the original plan to come to camp on the regularly scheduled pick-up day—a smart move since kids' moods can change quickly at camp. Enclosing some photos with the letter is a loving finishing touch.

When children write extremely homesick letters like the samples above, they often include a request to be picked up. What's the message there? On the surface, the message is: "I am (or was) homesick." Underneath, the message is, "I've lost confidence in myself." The severely homesick child is like a mountain climber who gets tired halfway up the mountain. The summit looks far away, and suddenly, the climber doesn't think he can make it. He has lost confidence. It's going to take someone else's empathy and encouragement for him to regain his confidence and climb the rest of the way to the top of the mountain. As a parent, you need to be that someone for your homesick child. Instill as much confidence as you can.

When children make it through a bout of homesickness and complete their planned stay at camp, they feel a tremendous sense of accomplishment.

After the first four days, I was sure that I couldn't make it through. I wrote to my parents on the second day of camp and told them to come pick me up. I really wanted to go home, but now I'm glad they didn't come get me. I just took things one day at a time, like my cabin leader told me. At home, I think I would have just been bored. I probably would have wanted to be back at camp. I'm definitely coming back to camp next summer, probably for a whole month, not just two weeks. —Rose, age 10

Electronic messages

Many camps now have facsimile machines and e-mail access, both of which allow faster written communication with your child. However, speed comes at the expense of personalizing. Sending your child a fax or an e-mail may make her feel more like a business colleague than your own flesh and blood. There is no substitute for a handwritten letter.

If you must fax or e-mail, either because you're sending an urgent message or because it's all you have time for, then be sure to verify the camp's policy and procedures for electronic messages. Many camps allow kids to receive faxes and e-mail, but do not allow them to send replies. The philosophy at most camps is that kids should be playing with each other and having fun, not sitting at a fax machine or a computer.

Don't have any illusions about how fast your fax or e-mail message may be getting to your child. We've visited some camps where the fax machine and computer in the central office are literally miles from the kids' cabins. Staff stopped by the central office only occasionally, and then they had to deliver the faxes or e-mails by hand. It was sometimes two days before children got their faxes, about the same time it takes to send a traditional letter.

Phone calls

As with faxes and e-mail, different camps have different policies about phone calls. Be sure you and your child understand the camp's phone policy before opening day. During camp, it's important to respect that policy because it's based on years of experience with what works and what doesn't work at that particular camp.

The experience at most camps, especially at those with more than 100 campers and sessions longer than one week, is that phone contact between parents and children makes homesickness worse. When a child hears his mom's or dad's voice, it can arouse a deep longing for home. For that reason, and because gaining independence is a chief goal of overnight camp, most do not allow children to talk to their parents on the phone except in rare emergencies. By comparison, the experience at other camps, especially ones with few campers and short sessions, is that phone contact between parents and children can be supportive and helpful. Such camps allow children to talk to their parents on the phone every day, if they wish.

Both philosophies have merit, and camp directors stand by them. However, no matter how you slice it, phone calls undermine campers' independence by breaking the continuity required for that independence. By contrast, letters take a few days to go back and forth, so they actually foster independence and offer support at the same time.

If your child's camp does allow phone calls, we recommend keeping them to a minimum. This will help ensure that your child gets the most out of his overnight camp experience. If the camp does not allow phone calls, don't ask the camp director to make an exception just for you, for a routine phone call. Instead, rely on traditional letters, postcards, and care packages for routine, heartfelt messages.

In a true emergency, such as the death of a family member, you should be allowed to talk with your child. Very few camps, if any, prohibit parents from talking to their children in dire emergencies. However, understand that it may take some time to get your child to the phone. Children can sometimes be involved in activities miles from the camp phone. If children are on an out-of-camp trip, they may even be completely inaccessible. For these reasons, it's common to have to leave a message with the camp staff to have your child call you back. This can be frustrating if the news is urgent and bad, but that's the reality of the situation.

Finally, don't panic if you get an unsolicited phone call from camp. It could be about something positive. Sometimes, camp staff will call to report how well things are going. These are fun phone calls to get. Other times, camp staff will call parents to enlist their help solving a complex behavioral or emotional problem. These are not such fun calls to get, but as a parent, you can offer valuable advice. Parents who receive a call from the camp about some problem their child is having generally feel grateful that the camp cares enough to inform them and enlist their assistance. Remember, the person you're talking to is a camping professional, but you are a parenting professional.

Care packages

Care packages are boxes of goodies (toys, clothes, magazines, etc.) that

families send to campers. Kids feel really special when they get a care package. It can even be something of a status symbol. Still, you shouldn't feel obligated to send a package to your son or daughter. Overnight camp is a huge gift in itself. High quality camps provide more than enough fun for each camper. If you do decide to mail your child

a care package, here are some tips on what to send and what not to send. Above all, remember to follow the camp's policy about what items campers are allowed to possess.

Size

The package should be reasonable in size. Sending a refrigerator-sized crate of treats is going to be expensive for you and embarrassing for your child. Keep the size reasonable, about the size of a shoe box. Kids should not expect to receive large, costly items at camp. The point is not to spoil them; it's simply to say, "I love you and I'm thinking about you."

Food, Candy, & Gum

Send only what the camp allows. Some camps allow campers to receive food, candy, and gum in the mail; others do not. Why? Food attracts animals and bugs. Also, without proper storage, food rots and becomes a health hazard. Don't put your child in an awkward position by smuggling food, candy, or gum to her if it's forbidden. It is especially frustrating for a camper to receive a nice batch of homemade cookies, only to have them confiscated.

Games, Toys, & Books

Games, toys, and reading material are excellent additions to any care package. Include some things that your child can share with his fellow campers.
You might send:

- miniature board games, like checkers or chess
- Frisbee® and other sorts of flying disks
- newspapers and magazines
- bean bag balls, such as Hackey Sacks®
- playing cards, and maybe poker chips
- Uno® and other sorts of card games
- choose-your-own-adventure books
- Nerf® balls and other sorts of sponge balls
- comic books, or the Comics section of the Sunday paper
- MadLibs® and other sorts of word games

You also might include an item or two that your child doesn't have to share, such as:

- a small stuffed animal
- markers and paper for drawing
- a disposable camera
- a novel
- origami paper and instructions
- a T-shirt
- a puzzle
- a baseball cap
- a blank scrapbook or journal to start at camp
- photos of the family

Commercial Care Packages

Although it will lack your personal touch, you can send your child a commercial care package. For about $30, commercial care package companies will send your child an age-appropriate, gender-appropriate combination of entertaining little toys, games, and knick-knacks. Because any care package is more special when another child hasn't received exactly the same thing, most of these companies are careful not to duplicate items sent to the same camp. (See *Resources & references* for a list of vendors.)

Birthdays

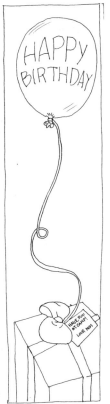

If your child's birthday happens during the camp session, make a celebration plan before she leaves. Some families celebrate birthdays before or after the camp session. That way, the whole family can get together and have a party, a special dinner, or some other kind of celebration. Other families arrange for their children to celebrate their birthdays at camp. Many camps are ready to accommodate these requests by providing a birthday cake and ice cream for your child and her cabin mates. Other camps simply sing "Happy Birthday" in the dining hall. If you and your child plan for her to celebrate her birthday at camp, find out ahead of time what that celebration will entail. Advanced planning will prevent disappointments.

All kids enjoy getting a small present on their actual birthday, especially if it happens during camp. Things that would otherwise go in a care package are perfect. Save any big, expensive presents until after camp is over. You wouldn't want anything really important to get lost, stolen, or broken. Plus, a treasure trove of fancy presents might make your child's fellow campers green with jealousy. Instead, send a birthday card, a modest care package, and a note reminding your child that he has presents waiting for him at home when camp is over.

Don't Send:

Money. Cash or checks can be lost or stolen. If you want your child to have money for a spending account at camp, send it to the camp directors. Most camps do not allow children to carry around cash, checks, credit cards, or bank cards. Verify the camp's policy.

Contraband. Basically, don't send anything that the camp forbids. Such contraband may include electronic games or appliances, knives, matches, lighters, or fireworks. It's probably not even a good idea to send squirt guns, cap guns, laser guns, or other types of toy guns. They may be confused for the real thing and create quite a disturbance.

Visiting camp

Visiting camp can bring your child great pleasure, of course. But be sure to come only when the camp allows. Some camps have a parents' weekend, where parents get to visit their children and see them perform some of the new skills they've learned. Other camps have a visiting day between sessions, so if your child is staying at camp for two consecutive sessions, you can visit for a day in between.

Visiting camp unannounced or on a day that has not been scheduled for visitation is a bad idea. More so than phone calls, in-person visits are an immediate form of contact that can provoke homesickness in your child and envy among her friends. Unscheduled visits are disruptive to campers' developing sense of independence. If you have any doubts about the appropriateness of your visit, be sure to call the camp and speak with the director.

What else is important to remember about visiting day?

- **Be on time.** Stick to what you promised on opening day. Your son or daughter will be counting on it.

- **Take a tour.** Your child would love to show you around camp. Keep any critical comments to yourself—this is your child's time to shine, not defend himself.

- **Keep an open mind.** You'll wonder about certain aspects of camp. Ask gently for an explanation before passing judgment. Praise all of your child's accomplishments.

- **Prepare for strong feelings.** Visiting day can be a wonderfully emotional time, but it's often hard for kids to say goodbye. Resist the temptation to offer your child a ride home. Instead, be understanding and encouraging. You'll see her again soon.

- **Share any sad news early and in person.** Telling your child about the death of a pet or sharing any other bad news is best done in person when you're there to provide comfort, not in a letter or a phone call. Break any bad news to your child early on visiting day to give you both time to talk about it.

- **Send a replacement if you'll be absent.** Your child wants to see you more than anyone else in the world. However, if you can't make it up for visiting day, tell your child far in advance. If possible, plan for a friend's parents to include your child in their own visiting day festivities.

Staying in touch with your child while she's at camp will bring you lots of vicarious pleasure. It's also a great source of entertainment and security for your son or daughter.

CHAPTER 14

Closing day

When we got picked up from camp in the summer of

1980, we had no idea that we would still be returning to the same place two decades later. Closing day is the end of one camp experience, but it can also be the beginning of something amazing. Perhaps it will be the beginning of a childhood enriched by yearly trips to camp, of ten or eleven months of longing for the next opening day, or, in some cases, of revisiting the process of choosing a camp. Although you will be delighted to be reunited with your son or daughter, jumping back into the car and speeding off may not be the best way to enjoy a smooth closing day. This chapter will guide you through that important final day of camp so you can soak it all in and plan for next year.

Plan the pickup

"I'm sorry. I thought closing day was tomorrow." Believe it or not, in our many years as cabin leaders, we have actually witnessed a few parents who didn't show up on closing day. It was devastating to their kids' sense of self-worth and trust in their parents. There's really no excuse for forgetting the date, but it happens. If your camp doesn't hand out reminders, write your own. If you've forgotten to do this, check the camp's information packet now or call the camp directly.

As with visiting day, getting picked up on time on closing day is a big deal to kids. Your camp will probably give you a time window of several hours. We recommend that you decide what hour in that window works best, and then follow through faithfully. If you agree that pick-up will be between 9:30 and 10:30, don't show up at noon. Your child had a great time at camp, and now she's eager to see you.

Now that we've restated our point about punctuality, we must also say that you should not show up before the camp's pick-up time starts. If the camp publishes a pick-up time slot of 9:00 a.m. to 12:00 p.m., don't drive in at 8:00 a.m. Campers and staff are extraordinarily busy before closing day and have planned to use their closing day time to pack, clean up, say good-bye to friends, and finish projects for parents. If you show up early, you might not even find your child because he's running around doing something. In that case, you haven't saved any time at all. Please be respectful of the camp's published pick-up time.

Plan to spend a little time at camp on closing day. You'll have administrative chores to complete, such as closing accounts, signing out, talking with the cabin leader, possibly checking with the medical staff, and combing through the lost-and-found. (Don't worry, staff members will be around to guide you through these steps.) Most important, many kids want to share their positive experiences, give their parents a tour of camp, and introduce new friends. Of course, some kids just want to get in the car and go, even though they had a great time.

It's difficult to predict how long you'll spend at camp on closing day, but don't count on anything less than an hour. Rushing into camp earlier than planned and announcing that you have to check out immediately so that you can make a 1:00 p.m. tee-time can add unnecessary trauma to the day. (Yes, we've heard parents use that tacky excuse.) You haven't spent time together as a family for a while. Plan to do so on closing day, and don't pack your schedule with other appointments.

What to expect from kids

Kids' reactions to being reunited with their parents are tough to predict, as we hinted earlier. Rather than predict your family's exact experience, let us share with you some typical reactions that we've seen over the years. These descriptions are a bit abstract. No child will behave exactly like these stereotypes, but it's helpful to know how widely kids' reunion behavior varies. Your child may show a combination of these responses.

The Gusher. Some kids will be very excited about their camp experience and will immediately want to describe everything about camp in two minutes. Parents will be drenched with a steady stream of stories and explanations that they may not completely understand. Not to worry. Gushers know that their parents are the most important people in their lives, so they want to share with them all the great things that happened. Whirlwind tours of important places and people are a common part of this sharing. Parents should just smile and go along for the ride (with a camera, of course!).

The Poker Face. These kids probably had a great time at camp, but are oddly quiet on closing day. They don't want to tell their parents much right away, but parents should not assume this is because they disliked camp. It's just that Poker Face kids have an especially hard time leaving. They may be a little depressed about leaving new friends and wonderful places. However, the stories and experiences, good or bad, will come out in time. Parents who want the scoop right away can spend a few extra minutes talking to the child's cabin leader.

The Tearful Camper. Some campers are visibly moved by the close of camp. Tears are a real testament to the power of the overnight camp experience. Indeed, a priceless moment for a cabin leader or a parent is witnessing a camper who cried when he arrived (because the separation was so hard) suddenly cry from sadness that he is leaving. Tearful Campers may want to leave quickly to avoid the awkwardness of the moment, or they may wish to linger. Parents should ask their child's preference or play the day by ear.

The Sensationalist. These kids immediately tell their parents the single most dramatic thing that happened to them during their camp stay. "When we were camping out, the tent stakes broke and it started to rain, and my sleeping bag got muddy, and then we heard thunder, and I thought we were gonna die!" Don't assume the worst. All campers have a mix of powerful positive and negative experiences at camp. Sensationalists may tell horror stories, but most of them had a great time at camp. Parents should listen carefully to get a balanced account of the session.

Debriefing your child's cabin leader

Regardless of how your child acts on closing day, it's always good to get an experienced adult perspective. The cabin leader is the best place to start. These conversations can be insightful, but you may have to probe to get the information you want. Most cabin leaders tend to smile a lot and tell parents that the session went well. Part of their job is to have a positive attitude. Nevertheless, all cabin leaders mentally evaluate the kids with whom they work. How could they not have some opinions based on a week or more of living with your child?

If you want a more thorough picture than what your child may tell you, experiment with some of the questions below. In some cases, the answers may not be ones you want to hear, but don't hold it against the cabin leader if you ask for an honest response and she gives it to you. Most parents appreciate the candor of another adult's opinion because they are always looking for ways to help their kids improve. However, if you don't want to know, don't ask.

Some cabin leaders, especially the young ones, may have difficulty telling you that your child was lazy, disrespectful, aggressive, or defiant. If you feel as if you're only getting sugar-coated pleasantries, but you suspect otherwise, try to make the leader feel at ease. Tell her why you are interested in any observations or suggestions that she might have about your child.

Good Questions to Ask Cabin Leaders:

- How did the session go?
- What did you enjoy most about the session?
- What were some of the biggest challenges you faced?
- I'm always looking for pointers. How did my child interact with the other kids in the cabin? What do you see as her strengths and weaknesses?
- Which activities did my child like best? How did her skills improve?
- Were there any discipline problems with my child? How were they handled?
- Was my child polite? Did she have good table manners? Did she eat and sleep well?

- Is there anything that you suggest we work on before next year at camp?

Tipping

This is a controversial topic. The expectation for tips varies widely from one camp to another. Many camps have a published "No Tipping" policy in their information packet. Cabin leaders at these camps are supposed to refuse tips from parents. In practice, however, a college student who is making a meager salary working at overnight camp is probably not going to turn down a twenty-dollar bill. Other camps don't mention tipping, but the cabin leaders expect it. Just like a server at a restaurant, these leaders feel disgruntled if they don't receive a tip.

To know best how to handle tipping, first check the camp's information packet. If there's a "No Tipping" policy, you need not give your child's cabin leader a cash tip, and he won't expect it. Of course, you can still tip him, or show your appreciation in other ways, if you're so inclined. Here are some examples:

- homemade baked goods
- something from your hometown
- that day's newspaper and/or a current magazine

You can also show your appreciation to the whole camp by donating:

- money to the camp facilities development or leadership training fund
- books to the camp library
- items for the staff lounge (old furniture, a coffee maker, rugs)

If the camp's information packet says nothing about tipping, you are not obligated to tip. However, it may be worthwhile to check with other parents, alumni, or the camp director about any unspoken tipping rules. It's rare for camps to have a published "pro-tipping" policy, but if yours does, that makes your decision easier. Remember, you always have the option of showing your appreciation in one of the non-traditional ways listed above.

Material objects are not the only way of showing appreciation. Indeed, what we most covet from parents is sincerity, plain and simple. Cabin leaders beam when parents take them aside, look them in the eyes, and say something like, "Jon, I know how hard you guys work. I just want you to know how much I appreciate that. My kid loves this place, and it's not because of the nice weather or the fun activities. It's because of people like you, who are sterling role models. You're doing important work here. Keep it up." Comments like that—moments of heartfelt thanks—are worth more than any sort of tip.

If closing day is too early to evaluate exactly how the overnight camp experience influenced your child, you can always delay the expression of your gratitude. Letters are a great way to thank a cabin leader or give valuable feedback to the camp director. Many camps even hand out exit questionnaires on closing day. These give families a chance to reflect on the session and provide constructive criticism. Send your comments back to camp as soon as you can, while the memories are fresh. Many directors read these notes and evaluations aloud at staff meetings to imbue additional enthusiasm and gratitude to cabin leaders.

Checking out

You arrived on time, gave your child a big hug, admired his crafts project, debriefed his cabin leader, and took a camp tour. What's left to do? Although each camp has a unique check-out protocol, you should, at a minimum, do the following:

1. **Gather all your child's belongings.** Check in, on, and around your child's cabin for clothes and other equipment. He probably has something under his bed or hanging on the back line that he's forgotten to pack. Use the equipment list you made while packing to verify you're returning home with all important items. Double-check the lost-and-found for anything that's still missing. It's better to search now than purchase an item for the second time once you return home.

2. **Give feedback to the camp director.** Closing day, like opening day, is hectic, but this may be your only opportunity to talk with the camp director face-to-face. It's helpful to share briefly both praise and constructive criticism. Although directors have many other parents with whom they need to talk, your comments will be remembered. You'd be surprised how one parent's brief comment to a director can revolutionize a camp's policy, program, or procedure. Remember, you are the reason the camp is in business.

3. **Debrief the medical staff.** If your child takes medicine or has special medical needs, you should talk to the camp nurse or doctor on closing day. Collect any left-over medicine and ask how things went. In the rare instance that your child was injured while at camp, it's a good idea to check with the medical staff to see whether they recommend any ongoing care or follow-up appointments with your family doctor. At high quality overnight camps, the medical staff will be readily accessible on closing day.

4. **Close your account.** At many overnight camps, there is some sort of account balance to settle at the end of each session. You may either owe money or be due money. Save yourself the paperwork and mailings by settling your account in person on closing day. This also gives you the opportunity to ask any questions you may have about your account, or buy some last-minute items at the camp store.

5. **Verify the mailing list.** Many camps enroll campers on a first-come, first-served basis. Therefore, you should verify that the camp has your correct mailing address for next year's registration forms. If you have questions about when next year's registrations are due, be sure to ask. One day could make the difference between securing a spot in the session you want and getting put on the waiting list.

6. **Sign-out.** Actually putting your signature on some kind of sign-out list verifies for the camp that kids' legal guardians are taking them out of camp. Because of the minute risk that an unauthorized adult might leave camp with a child, many high quality camps have official sign-out lists.

Your child has now experienced the joys and benefits of overnight camping, and you both have some time to reflect on the experience. You'll

notice some positive changes in your child right away. Other changes will take time to develop and manifest themselves. Make no mistake about it. Camp has done your child a world of good.

BELLS & WHISTLES

Just for kids

The American Camping Association uses the slogan
"Camp Gives Kids a World of Good." Unlike most advertisements, this one is true. Camp will be one of the happiest times of your life. One of our grandfathers says that summer camp was the best time of his life! We agree. That's why we've been at camp each summer for the past 20 years. Although we're not campers anymore, we love being part of the camp staff. Today, our favorite thing about camp is sharing it with young people like you.

Enjoying camp
We believe that what you put into camp is what you get out of it. The harder you try, the more fun you'll have. That's why the next section contains our top seven tips for enjoying camp. The section after that will help you maximize your fun at camp by listing the best ways to deal with homesick feelings. When you're done reading this chapter, you'll know more than most kids about getting the most out of camp.

1. Pay attention at orientation.
Orientation is a speech, full of information about the camp. It usually happens on the first day. Sometimes one staff member talks to the whole camp. Other times, each cabin leader gives a short talk to his own cabin. Camps have orientations because there's a lot to tell you about the activities, rules, and schedules at camp. At orientation, you'll learn stuff

like where the courts, fields, and bathrooms are. You'll also learn what time games, meals, and free swims happen. Without an orientation you might feel kind of lost because camp is a completely new place. Listen and learn. If you forget something, just ask your cabin leader.

2. Learn your way around camp.

If you're lucky, your camp may give all new campers a tour on the first day. Someone who knows the campgrounds will show you all of the places at camp. You'll feel more comfortable when you know your way around, so we recommend taking the tour. If your camp doesn't offer a tour on the first day, ask your cabin leader, one of your instructors, or a second-year camper to show you and your new friends around. Some camps even have a map of the campgrounds. You came to camp to have fun, not to wander around looking for stuff.

3. Make friends.

Making friends is one of the best things about overnight camp. The friends you make at camp might be your friends for the rest of your life. Without friends, camp might get boring. To make friends at camp, remember to tell people your name. Say, "Hi, my name is . . . " (and then say your name). Hold out your hand to shake hands. Squeeze your new friend's hand firmly, and look him in the eye. Say, "It's nice to meet you."

Talking about camp is an easy way to make friends. Say, "How did you find out about this camp?" or "What year at camp is this for you?" Tell people where you are from. Say, "I'm from . . . " (and then say your home town). Ask, "Where are you from?"

Another good way to make friends is by playing. Think of a game you can share, and then find some other kids who want to play. Good sharing games are Frisbee®, catch, tag, jump-rope, H-O-R-S-E, and cards. You can also start pick-up games of basketball or another sport you like. If you brought a neat game from home, find some other kids who want to play with you. If other kids are already playing a game, watch for a while so that you understand the rules, then ask whether you can join in.

4. Stay busy.

Some kids forget how important it is to stay busy at camp. They walk around, get bored, and miss home. Believe us, you'll have much more fun at camp if you stay busy and go to all your favorite activities.

There are probably a lot of activities at camp that you don't have at home, so check them out! You'll have plenty of time to sit around when you get home. At camp, it's best to stay busy. Our cabin leaders used to tell us, "Don't vegetate . . . motivate!"

5. Try new things.

This might be your first time at overnight camp, or maybe you've been before. Either way, there will be something new to try. There will be new people to meet and play with.

Some kids think, "I haven't tried that activity, but I know I won't like it." Maybe they're right or maybe they're wrong. Maybe they think they won't like it, but they love it once they try it. You won't know until you try. Be adventurous! Go out and try new things at camp. It's one of the best ways to have fun.

Strange Camp Names...
Where do they come from?

Camp people are pretty silly when it comes to naming things. At our camp, we call the people who set the table "slingers." We don't know why. That's just what we call them. We call a bathroom a "scollege" because in the old days they named them after different colleges, like Harvard and Yale. Funny names are one of the things that make camp special.

Some names aren't funny, but they do sound different. Many of these different-sounding names are traditional. They tell you something about the camp's history or heritage. For example, Camp Masqua is named after a Native American chief. Where did your camp's name come from?

6. Be creative.

Whether you go to a computer camp or a sports camp, you will always have the chance to be creative. Create a new computer game. Create a new soccer play. Create a piece of art to bring home to your family. Create a spooky story to tell your friends around the campfire. Create a new kind of jump off the diving board. At camp, you'll have lots of chances to be creative. It's a good feeling to make something new and share it with other people.

7. Set a good example.

The way you act at camp can determine how much fun you have. If you listen and follow directions, you'll have more fun. You'll make friends and earn the respect of your cabin leader. Other people will treat you kindly, and that feels good.

On the other hand, if you break rules and goof off all the time, things will be different. It will be hard to make friends. Your cabin leader may

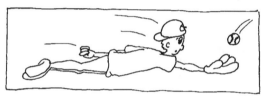

take privileges away from you. Other people won't want to be nice to you if you're not nice to them, and that feels bad.

Have you ever heard of the Golden Rule? The Golden Rule is: *Treat other people the way you want them to treat you.* If you want other people to be nice to you, then you have to be nice to them. The Golden Rule is true at camp just like anywhere else. Try to set a good example for other people to follow. You will have more fun at camp, and you might also teach other kids how to have more fun.

Homesick feelings are normal

Before I went to camp, I practiced staying overnight at my best friend's house. That helped me get used to not seeing my mom and dad every day.
—Marian, age 9

You can't make homesickness go away for good. For me, a little bit is always there, in the back of my mind. But I learned what to do so homesick feelings don't bother me.
—John, age 9

Overnight camps are made for kids to have fun. Most kids love it, but almost all kids feel a little bit homesick, just like Marian and John did. It's normal to feel a little sad or nervous when you're away from home. And even though homesickness feels bad, those feelings mean something good. Homesick feelings mean that you love your parents and your home. Regular homesick feelings don't bother most kids. But if your homesick feelings are strong, and they start to bother you, there are lots of things you can think and do to feel better. Doing these things now prevents you from having strong homesick feelings later. Try them before camp starts.

1. Think positively.

Camp will be a blast! You already know that there will be lots of new activities to try, cool people to hang out with, and different places to go. If your camp has its own property, there will also be some beautiful nature to explore.

A whole session at camp may seem like a long time. But, hey, two or four weeks isn't really that much time to spend at camp. If you're nine years old, you've already lived more than 468 weeks. What's only two weeks? Even eight weeks seems like a short time when you remember how many weeks you've been alive. Camp will go quickly because of all the fun you'll be having. You might even wish you could stay longer.

2. Encourage your parents.

Did you know that some parents get a little nervous about overnight camp? Well, they do. It's normal. They're nervous because they love you and they want you to have fun. Tell them you *will* have fun. Camp will be a fun challenge. While you're at camp, your parents should do some fun stuff too, like read books and visit with their grown-up friends.

3. Plan your time at camp.

It's helpful to get a calendar and look at it with your parents. Turn to the month when camp starts. Mark the day you will leave and the day you will return. Count the number of days you'll be at camp and color them in. That way, you and your parents can see exactly how long you'll be gone. Maybe you'll also want to count how many weeks it is from now until you leave. Knowing when camp is coming up really makes kids and parents feel comforted. The fewer surprises, the better.

4. Get to know your camp.

Camp has a special culture. The schedules and customs are different from the ones you have at school and at home. There's probably a certain time when everyone has to wake up in the morning, and certain times for meals. You may get to choose some activities, and other activities might be planned for you. Even the food might be a little different from what you're used to. Most kids love camp food.

There are lots of places to learn about your camp. First of all, your camp should send you some papers to read and pictures to look at. Some camps also have video tapes and CD-ROMs that tell about the camp. If you have a camp video or CD-ROM, check it out. Maybe your camp even has a web page you can visit. When you look at all these pictures of camp, what looks good? What's different about camp, compared to home?

If you still have questions about the camp before you go, ask your parents or call the camp on the phone. The more you learn about your camp ahead of time, the more comfortable you will feel once you get there. If you feel right at home at camp, you won't miss your real home as much!

5. Spend some practice time away from home.

Spending two or three days at a friend's or relative's house helps you get used to being away from home. It gives you some practice knowing what camp will be like. If you miss home during your short trip, try some "anti-homesickness" strategies from the "Things That Help Homesickness" list on page 207.

During your practice trips, you should also keep in touch with your family in the same way you will at camp: by writing letters. Try not to use the phone at all. Most camps don't allow campers to use the phone. In your letters, write about what fun things you did that day, what the weather was like, and what was on your mind. Seal the letter in an envelope, address it, stamp it, and mail it just like you will at camp.

6. Pack something special from home.

You'll be packing a lot of different things to bring to camp. Besides all the regular supplies, many kids like to pack something special from home. This could be a photograph of your family, a drawing of your pet, a penny with your birth year on it, a small stuffed animal, your favorite pillow, a little toy, or anything else that reminds you of home. What do you think you might like to bring? Pick something that's not too valuable, in case it gets lost.

7. Read a story about overnight camp.

There are some good stories about overnight camp. Two that we like are *Off to Camp*, by Myra Pravda, and *Wish You Were Here*, by Martina Selway. You can find these books, and maybe others like them, at a bookstore or library. You can also order them on-line, but ask your parents first. Reading about how other kids enjoy overnight camp will take away some of the mystery. You'll feel even more excited about going!

YIKES!
No Nintendo, Sega, or PlayStation?

At most overnight camps, video games are not allowed. Camp is a time to get back to nature. Don't worry. You'll survive.

Did you ever wonder why kids love video games so much? One reason is because it gives them a sense of "mastery." You feel really good when you win your favorite game. This increases your "self-esteem." You feel good about yourself. That's nice, but how does it work?

Well, video games give you a lot of real (not imaginary) control over something in your life. Control is something we all enjoy. Control is especially important to kids, because you live in a world mostly controlled by grown-ups.

In a video game, no one tells you what to do. *You* shoot the alien invaders, *you* discover the secret door at the end of the hall, and *you* win the race. Video games reinforce your skills and enthusiasm and provide constant challenges, such as the boiling lava pit on Level 93.

Camp does all this same great stuff...well, without the boiling lava. Instead, camps are in real, natural settings that teach kids about sports, art, and friendship. The independence and self-esteem you gain won't be spoiled by electrical blackouts, computer glitches, or soda pop in the joystick.

It will be good to take a break from video games for a while. Don't you think?

If your homesick feelings bother you while you're at camp, try thinking and doing what's on the following list of "Things That Help Homesickness." See what works best for you. Maybe you can even invent some ways to make your homesickness better that aren't on the list. Avoid stuff from the list of "Things That Do NOT Help Homesickness."

To give you a head start, here are the two things work for almost *all* kids who feel a little homesick:

• **Do a Fun Activity**

• **Talk with Your Cabin Leader**

Like we said before, cabin leaders enjoy talking with kids. That's one reason they choose to work at overnight camps. But your cabin leader can't read your mind. If you're feeling bad on the inside, it might not show on the outside. You need to tell him if you're feeling bad. No matter what he is doing, he's never too busy to talk with you. He can give you lots of suggestions for how to feel better and have more fun at camp.

As the old saying goes, "Time flies when you're having fun." It's true. Before you know it, your camp stay will be done, and you'll be packing up your stuff and heading home. You'll notice that you feel proud and happy. Maybe you'll be back next summer to see your new friends. We're sure you'll have a great time!

Kids know the best ways to deal with homesick feelings during camp

We asked more than 1,000 kids what they thought and did to cope with homesick feelings. Some things helped, but other things didn't. Here's what all those kids said about getting over their homesickness.

Things That Help Homesickness:	What Kids Said:
1. Do something fun.	*When I felt a little homesick, I just tried to stay busy. I did something with one of my friends, or I went to an activity. When I was doing something fun, I wasn't thinking about home, so I wasn't homesick.*
	—Mark, age 8

Things That Help Homesickness:	**What Kids Said:**
2. Do something to feel closer to home.	*There's a lot I do at camp to feel closer to home. I hang out with friends from home, I write lots of letters to my parents, and I look at the picture of my family that I brought. Some kids don't like to look at family pictures because it makes them feel more homesick, but it works for me.* —Sarah, age 9
3. Think about the good side of being at camp.	*For me, looking on the bright side means thinking about all the fun things to do at camp. At home, I can't do archery or sailing. We have a pool, but the lake here at camp is better. Plus, there are more friends to play with at camp than at home. When I remember all the things I have at camp that I don't have at home, I don't feel so homesick.* —Phillip, age 11
4. Try to be happy and have fun.	*When I have homesick feelings, I just change the way I feel. I mean, sometimes homesickness can feel bad, but actually be good. It means that you love your parents, and that's a good thing. So while I'm at camp, I just try to be happy and have fun.* —José, age 12
5. Remind yourself that your stay at camp is not that long after all and that you'll be home pretty soon.	*What do I think or do when I feel homesick? Well, I tell myself that four weeks is pretty short. I mean, I've already been here a week, and it's gone by really fast. School lasts thirty-nine weeks and camp lasts only four. When I remember how short camp is, I know I can make it through. I don't get that homesick actually.* —Natalie, age 9
6. Talk with someone who can make you feel better.	*Sometimes when you feel homesick, you feel really alone. I mean, there's lots of people around at camp, but you still feel like you're the only one who is homesick. When I talked to my cabin leader, she told me that it was normal. I found out that almost every kid feels a little homesick at camp. After I talked to Sima I felt a lot better. She helped me think of ways to make my homesick feelings go away.* —Kath, age 13

Things That Do NOT Help Homesickness	**What Kids Said:**
1. Sitting around doing nothing.	*The more I sat around, the worse I felt. I just thought about home and started feeling sorry for myself. It seemed like time went by so slowly.* —Fred, age 9
2. Giving up.	*I thought there was nothing I could do to make my homesickness better. It was like, 'OK, I feel this way and I'm always gonna feel this way.' I didn't know what to think or do to make things better.* —Mollie, age 8
3. Wishing that things were different.	*I just wished that I never felt homesick at all. And I wished that things at camp were more like things at home. I wished my parents would just come and get me right away. It didn't help.* —Charlie, age 11
4. Doing something to try to get back home on your own.	*I thought about running away, but then I realized how dangerous that would be, like hitchhiking or something. What if some crazy person picked me up? After I talked with my cabin leader, I realized that wouldn't help my homesickness and it wouldn't be safe. I was lucky, though. My cabin leader gave me a lot of good ideas for feeling less homesick. Some of them really work.* —Ana, age 10
5. Doing something angry or mean to try to get sent home.	*I thought about trying to break a camp rule to get sent home, but then I realized it wouldn't help my homesickness. If I got in trouble, I'd probably just feel worse. Instead, I talked to my counselor, and that was pretty cool.* —Hsin, age 13
6. Spending time by yourself.	*A lot of times I just like to go up to the top of Hall Lodge and think. It's really pretty up there. But if I'm feeling homesick, it's not good for me to be alone. I just end up thinking a lot about my parents, and that makes it worse. Instead, I try to find some friends and just hang out together. We like to sing.* —Laurie, age 9

Get Ready To Go

And Beat the Homesickness Monster

- Practice walking around your yard or house at night with a flashlight. Wear shoes or sandals, just like you will at camp.

- Practice talking with other kids and adults about how you feel. Tell them what's on your mind!

- Bring something special from home to camp, if you think it will make you feel good.

- Bring pre-stamped and pre-addressed envelopes, so you'll be ready to write letters.

- Pack and shop for camp with your parents. When kids and parents prepare together, it's more fun.

- Go over the opening day of camp in your head. When will you leave the house? Who will be coming in the car? The fewer surprises, the better. If plans do change, go with the flow.

- Read the list of Things That Help Homesickness and pick your favorite strategies.

Guidelines for considering a shortened stay

Shortened stays are very, very rare, which is why this is a short section. At camps where we've worked, fewer than 1 child in 100 returns home early because of extreme homesickness or a severe behavior problem. However, deciding on a shortened stay must be done carefully, which is why we've included this information. If you don't anticipate a problem, you need not read any further. If a problem develops later, you can always come back and read more.

There are times when homesick feelings are so strong, and last for so many days, that the best thing to do is shorten the child's camp stay and have her return home early. How strong is too strong? How many days are too many? These important questions must be answered individually. Decisions about shortened stays should be made on a case-by-case basis. What your child can tolerate might be too much for another child.

The keys in every case of a shortened camp stay are to make the decision carefully and frame the decision to return home positively. There are eight steps parents should go through, and they are the same for every case of extreme homesickness or severe behavior or emotional problems. We refer to homesickness throughout this chapter because that's the most common reason for a shortened stay.

1. Discuss the severity of the homesickness.

In cases of severe homesickness, you will somehow become aware of your child's distress. Either he will write to you, or a member of the camp staff will contact you. If what you're hearing tells you that a shortened camp stay should be considered, get clear on the severity of your child's homesickness. Talk to the camp director and your child's cabin leader on the phone and ask these specific questions:

Safety and Severity
- How safe is he being? Is he threatening to run away or do something else unsafe, or has he been following the camp rules and listening to his cabin leader?

- How upset does he look? Is he crying most the time, or does he look as if he is having fun most of the time?

- How is his mood? Is he happy most of the time, or is he often sad, down, or lonely? During quiet times, is he calm or anxious?

- How long has his homesickness lasted? Is this a one-day phenomenon, or has he been homesick for more than a few days?

Activity

- How much interest or pleasure does he show in activities?

- Does he seem tired and lack energy most of the time?

Eating and Sleeping

- How is his appetite? Is he eating full, balanced meals at mealtime, or is he barely eating?

- How is he sleeping? Is he getting a good night's sleep, or does he have trouble falling asleep or staying asleep most nights?

Social Functioning

- How are his friendships? Is he playing with other children, or is he usually alone?

- How is his homesickness affecting the other kids in his group? Is it not a problem, or is his distress starting to make other kids unhappy or frustrated?

- How is his homesickness affecting his cabin leader's time? Is the problem taking up a significant amount of time, or is this only a minor inconvenience?

Coping Skills

- How are his coping skills? Is he making an effort to think and do different things to help his homesickness, or has he given up, claiming that nothing will help?

- How is his attitude? Does he desperately want to go home, or is he interested in trying to make it through to the end of camp?

Extreme homesickness is rare, but it sometimes happens. Answering these questions will help you determine whether your child is extremely homesick, or just challenged by normal feelings of missing home. There's no magic formula. You and the camp staff must use your best judgment. Decide together whether you should consider a shortened stay.

2. Share your position on shortened stays.

It's helpful for the camp staff to know what your position is on shortened stays. They can work with your child more effectively when they know what the options are. If coming home early is simply not an option, the camp staff will do their best to help your child cope with her homesickness. If coming home early is an option, the camp staff has something to fall back on if they decide your child's homesickness is too extreme for her to stay at camp.

3. Resist talking directly to your child, but have the cabin leader keep him informed.

Very seldom do camps allow homesick children to talk on the phone with their parents. Such conversations often make the homesickness worse and result in hasty decisions to bring the child home early. Children and parents invariably regret these hasty decisions because afterwards they wonder whether they could have done something else to solve the problem. Returning home early is the last resort in cases of severe homesickness. It should be done only after all other options have been tried.

We recommend that you not talk directly to your homesick child. Hearing your voice will open emotional floodgates and make it nearly impossible for you to reason with him or convince him to stay. However, we do recommend that the cabin leader tell your child that the two of you have spoken. Why? First of all, it's important for extremely homesick children to know that the camp staff is taking their distress seriously. When children know their parents have been contacted, they know their feelings are being taken seriously. That's comforting. Second, it can be a huge relief for severely homesick children to know that a shortened stay is possible. Sometimes, this relief helps alleviate their homesickness, and a shortened stay no longer needs to be considered.

Unfortunately, knowing that a shortened stay is possible can also backfire. Some children will use this option as a crutch, and give up coping altogether. They stay homesick because they see their distress as a ticket home. Nevertheless, no one should get angry at a child who chooses this route. If you want your child to try spending time away from home again, you'll need to be supportive. Sometimes this means being supportive even when you think your child could have tried harder.

4. Give it time.

At this point, you have already talked with the camp director and your child's cabin leader. Let's say that together you've decided that your child indeed does have a case of extreme homesickness, and that coming home early is a realistic option. Our recommendation is: Don't make a decision right away. Ask your child's cabin leader to work with your child for another day or two on ways of coping with his homesickness. Then, plan a specific time when you will talk again with the cabin leader to get an update.

For example, you might say, "O.K., at this point, we have a contingency plan. Ben could come home if things don't get better for him soon. You'll call me at work on Tuesday at 2:00 o'clock and we'll discuss how he's doing."

5. Make sure your child wants to come home.

When the cabin leader calls back, ask whether your child's homesickness has improved. If you and the cabin leader feel your child is still severely homesick and should come home, make sure the cabin leader has asked him whether he definitely wants to go home. Some kids will have improved and will want to stay at camp; others will be adamant about returning home. It is important for your child to be involved in this decision. You wouldn't want to surprise him if you came to pick him up.

6. Make a final decision and frame it positively.

If your child is still terribly homesick after days of trying to cope, and days of getting help from the camp staff, the right thing to do may be to allow him to come home early. If this is his desire, you can bet he'll be relieved. Nevertheless, this is a difficult time for your child. He can easily view his early return home as a personal failure. The crucial element of turning his shortened stay into a success is to frame it positively. You and the camp staff need to tell your child how proud you are that he made it through at least part of camp.

You might say, "Lewis, I think it's great that you made it this far at overnight camp. This was one of your first times away from home and you did a great job. This summer you made it through 6 days; maybe next summer you'll make it through all 14 days. You have a lot to be proud of."

Cabin leaders should also know to give similar positive messages to your child. Whenever we're talking to a child who is about to return home early, we give him lots of praise for trying so hard. We remind him of all the different ways of coping that he learned. We remind him of the fun times he had. (There are always at least a few fun times to reminisce about.) We tell him that we hope we'll see him next year, and that he should be proud to have gotten so far through the session. We privately remember that camp isn't for every child. There are some children who just don't like it. Camp should never be a jail. It should be fun and safe.

7. Be discrete with the pick-up at camp.

In most cases of a shortened stay, a family member picks the child up at camp. This pick-up should be discrete, meaning not in front of many other campers. The pick-up is usually an emotional moment, with everyone having lots of mixed feelings. An emotional reunion between a child and his family is a hard thing for other kids to witness. They sometimes wish that someone from their own family would come pick them up, or at least visit. For that reason, pick your child up at a time when the camp staff tells you there won't be much going on. Rest hour and free time are generally good bets, but always have the cabin leader recommend exactly when and where you should pick your child up.

8. Be decisive about your plan.

Don't change your mind after visiting with your child for a while at camp. Of course he will be acting less homesick because you're standing right there. But that doesn't mean he suddenly can make it through the rest of the session. Changing your mind about a shortened stay, even if your child agrees at that moment, can have disastrous consequences.

We've seen parents and severely homesick kids visit for a while and then change their minds about leaving camp early. Yet, as soon as the parents drove away, the kids lapsed back into extreme homesickness. The next day, the parents had to drive back to camp. Leaving camp early is not an easy decision to make. Don't make it harder by changing your mind at the last minute. Be decisive, and praise all of your child's efforts.

Because of the impact a shortened stay can have on your child's self-esteem, attitudes about overnight camp, and attitudes about future separations, it's important to make such a decision slowly, thoughtfully, and in close collaboration with the camp staff.

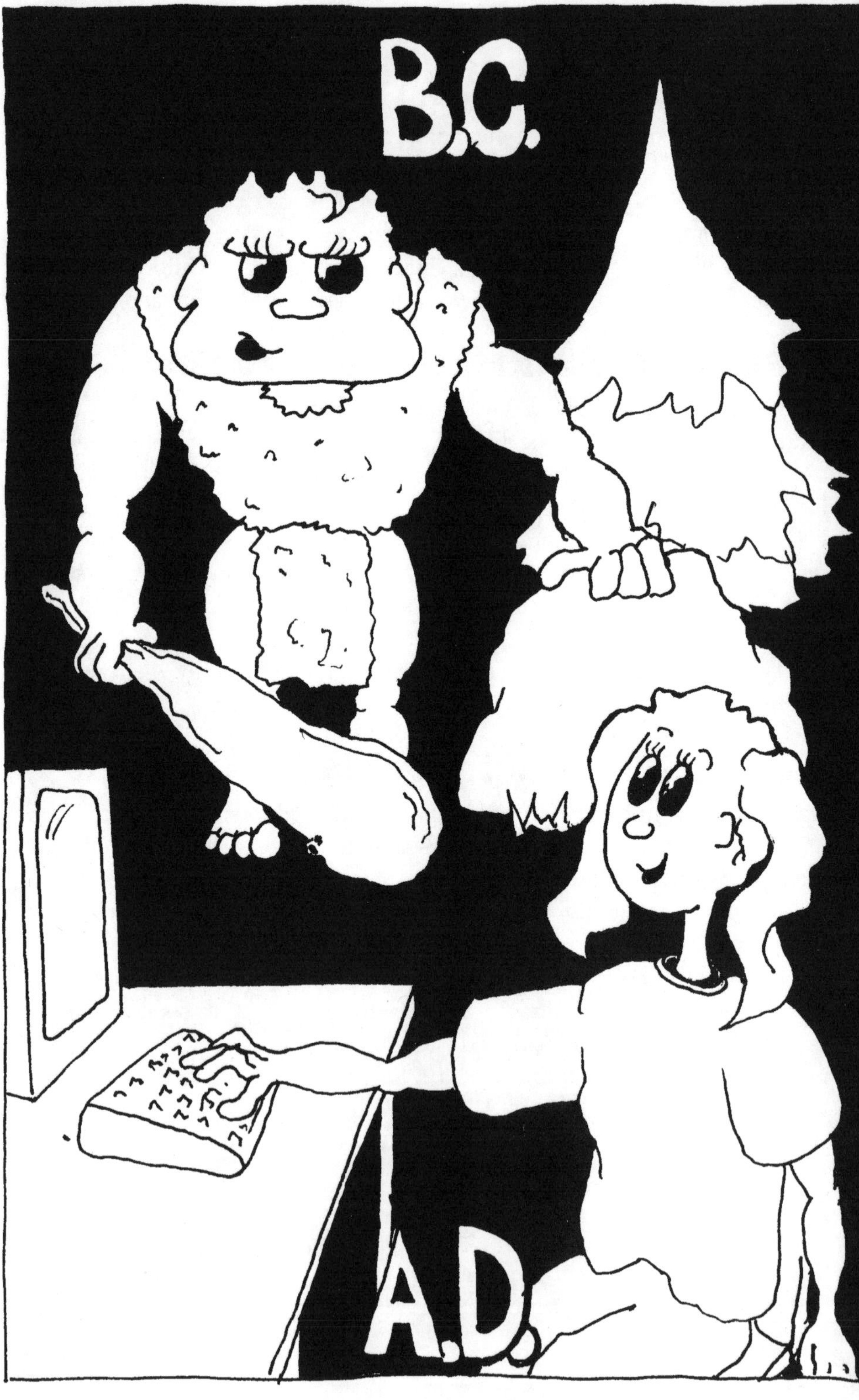
B.C.
A.D.

A short history of overnight camping

If you think about it, overnight camping is a somewhat strange concept. As civilization evolved, people built cities to shield themselves from the savage wilderness. Why, then, would people pay money to leave the safety of civilization and go back into the wilderness? Because city folk increasingly appreciated the beauty of nature and the wholesome purity of country living. Organized camping in the United States was a response to growing urbanization. Parents wanted their children to spend school vacations in lush natural settings that promoted physical, mental, and spiritual health.

> *In cultivating general morality and kindly behavior the camps are helped*
> *chiefly through their usefulness in making boys strong vitally, in improving*
> *their power of digestion, in increasing their lung capacity, in letting the*
> *sunshine pour upon every portion of their bared bodies.*
> —Dr. Winthrop Tisdale Talbot, 1905

Early camping

William Frederick Gunn and his wife Abigail are said to be the originators of organized overnight camping. The Gunns were headmasters of the Gunnery School, a private school in Connecticut. In the summer of 1861, they took a group of students into the wilderness along Long Island Sound for two weeks. At this original summer camp, activities included hiking, boating, fishing, and sailing.

Early campers, like those at the Gunnery Camp, played sports, told stories, and learned about living in the outdoors. There were some big differences though, between early overnight camps and the ones we have today. Instead of driving or flying, some kids had to travel by train for several days to get to camp. Fancy sports facilities were rare and some activities, such as water-skiing, didn't even exist. Toilets were rare, and campers often had to dig their own latrines. Camps were also generally more religious than they are now. In part, this was because the YMCA, a traditionally Christian organization, sponsored many early camps.

The popularity of camps grew quickly. Only a few dozen camps were operating by the 1880s, but by 1900, that number had grown to several hundred. Most of the early camps, many of which are still operating, were located in the Northeast and upper Midwest.

It's not fair, but boys got to go to camp first. Fortunately, by about 1910, when the American Camping Association began, more girls' camps had formed. Over the next few decades, camps evolved into something similar to what we have today. About 50% of the camps in America are coed, 30% are all-girls, and 20% are all-boys.

Cultural influences

Military traditions and Native American culture both influenced early camps. Groups such as the Boy Scouts, founded by Lord Baden-Powell in 1908, adopted military structures, as did many camps sponsored by the Scouts. Bugle calls, uniforms, mess halls, and military-style daily schedules became part of most overnight camps. These military traditions are still in use at many camps across the country. Most camps that keep these traditions don't try to be Army boot camps for kids. However, the military legacies have survived because a regimented structure is indispensable to  managing the activities and whereabouts of hundreds of children.

The biggest proponent of Native American culture in camping was Canadian-American naturalist, artist, and author Ernest Thompson Seton (1860-1946). Seton had been an early pioneer in the Boy Scouts, but after living with Native American tribes for many years, he decided to pursue and promote a different approach to camping. With the blessings of his host tribes, Seton took it upon himself to visit many camps and promote his organization, the Woodcraft League of America, which celebrated Native American values for all Americans. Seton's books and practices became well-known in the camping world. At one point, the Woodcraft League of America, established in 1902, was even more popular than the Scouts. Its influences remain strong in the Scouts, the YMCA, Camp Fire Boys and Girls and many camping movements abroad.

Woodcraft teaches young people how to survive in the woods, respect nature, and live harmoniously with all of God's creations. Today, fewer than a dozen camps in America still perform the weekly Woodcraft ceremony as designed by Seton and his Native American friends. Although many camps continue to use Native American names, motifs, and costumes in their programs, this cultural assimilation ranges from the respectful to the absurd. Despite drifting away from authentic Native American traditions, many camps still have a natural setting and an educational philosophy that promotes healthy environmental values.

Wartime years

Camping continued to grow rapidly throughout the first half of the 20th century. Before World War II, camping was seen as a natural extension of the educational system, a way for young people to use the summer months to build useful skills. Academic subjects were routinely taught, and campers could get tutoring from the staff, most of whom were local college students.

During this period, camping became less of an exclusively middle-class activity. Parents of all classes saw camping as beneficial to child development, not just as a retreat from the evils of the city. In 1922, Harvard University President Charles W. Eliot declared, "The organized summer camp is the most important step in education that America has given the world."

In the two decades after World War II, from about 1945 to 1965, overnight camping in the United States became increasingly popular. According to camping historian Eleanor Eells, the adventuresome spirit of a relieved post-war society, a growing economy, and the baby boom all contributed.

Strong moral development was always a goal of those who promoted the camping movement. However, this goal shifted somewhat in light of World War II, the Korean War, and the increasingly hostile Cold War. Adults focused their attention on preparing children to be citizens in an ever-changing world.

[Opportunities must be provided] for campers to learn to do for themselves, to practice outdoor skills that teach self-reliance and resourcefulness. This should happen in daily living, not on an occasional hike or outing, and the camper should have an active part in the preparations. These are not times

of entertainment, but times of doing, and from the day-to-day practice will come skills that will serve naturally in times of emergency.
—camping enthusiast C. I. Hammett, 1951

While somewhat patriotic, this statement should not be interpreted as a desire to train kids at camp to be soldiers. Hammett also wrote that the goal of camping should be to develop future citizens and provide children the opportunity to get to know and understand other children of different racial, ethnic, religious, geographic, and economic groups. In the early 1950s, this was a rather progressive idea in the United States. These days, more and more camps have international staff and campers, as well as a mix of children from different backgrounds.

Overnight camping today

Camps across the country began closing several decades ago for a variety of reasons. In the late 1960s and early 1970s, there was a sharp decline in

the camper-aged population as the baby-boomers grew up. Fewer campers needed fewer camps. At the same time, many camps became so valuable as vacation property that the taxes became unaffordable. Sadly, some outstanding camps couldn't afford to stay in business.

In the 1980s and 1990s, the children of the babyboomers started going to camp and once again enrollment surged. However, there was a decline in the number of new residential camps, and some old camps went bankrupt or sold out to real-estate developers. For example, the Lake Winnipesaukee region of New Hampshire, long a hearth of overnight camping in New England, once had about 100 camps along its shores. Today, there are about 25.

Demographics and economics were not the only reasons that the number of overnight camps dipped. Campers themselves began to request shorter stays. This meant that, in order to fill a camp for the whole summer, directors needed three to eight times the number of campers. In the past, it had been common for campers to spend the entire summer at camp, usually seven or eight weeks. A camp with 100 beds needed only

100 boys or girls to complete enrollment. However, as family vacations, specialty camps, special needs camps, and other summer opportunities for kids increased, camper stays shortened. Today, a camp with 100 beds might need 500 or more children to complete enrollment over an eight-week summer.

Paradoxically, more children go to overnight camp than ever before. In 1999 , the American Camping Association reported the number of children attending day and overnight camps in the United States to be nearly nine million. Indeed, there was an 8-10% increase in summer camp enrollment each year between 1992 and 1999. Why? Partly because there are now more camper-age children, partly because camps are more accessible to low-income children and children with disabilities, and partly because children are staying for fewer weeks. According to the ACA, "the most popular session length of camp is one week, followed by two weeks, then a month." Along with the trend toward shorter stays, there has also been a trend toward coeducational camping.

. . .

Our fathers and grandfathers lament the fact that their traditional camps have been torn down and replaced with condominiums. Sometimes the dollar value of lakefront property is worth more to some people than priceless memories and the spiritual growth of children. However, in many important ways, camping hasn't changed a bit. The core ideas and ideals—indeed the very goals of overnight camping that William and Abigail Gunn first institutionalized—remain alive and well in high quality camps today.

Resources & references

This final section includes information on these camp resources and references, in the following order:

1. National camping organizations & camp-affiliated organizations
2. Internet web sites for finding camps
3. American Camping Association section offices
4. Canadian camping contacts
5. Resources for finding special needs camps
6. Commercial care package vendors
7. Name labels, laundry bags, and other camp supplies
8. Resource books

1. National camping organizations & camp-affiliated organizations

Many of these national organizations have regional or local branches. To obtain information on the branch, chapter, or counsel nearest you, call the national centers or visit the national web sites listed below.

American Camping Association

address:	5000 State Road 67 North
	Martinsville, IN 46151-7902
phone:	765-342-8456
fax:	765-342-2065
Internet:	www.ACAcamps.org

Association of Jewish Sponsored Camps

address:	130 East 59th Street
	New York, NY 10022
phone:	212-751-0477
fax:	212-755-9183
e-mail:	info@jewishcamps.org
Internet:	www.jewishcamps.org

Boy Scouts of America

address:	1325 West Walnut Hill Lane
	P.O. Box 152079
	Irving, TX 75015-2079
phone:	972-580-2401
fax:	972-580-2413
Internet:	www.bsa.scouting.org

Camp Fire Boys and Girls

address:	4601 Madison Avenue
	Kansas City, MO 64112-1278
phone:	816-756-1950
fax:	816-756-0258
Internet:	www.campfire.org

Christian Camping International/USA

address:	P.O. Box 62189
	Colorado Springs, CO 80962
phone:	719-260-9400
fax:	719-260-6398
Internet:	www.gospelcom.net/cci/

Easter Seals

address:	230 West Monroe Street
	Suite 1800
	Chicago, IL 60606
phone:	800-221-6827/312-726-6200
TDD:	312-726-4258
fax:	312-726-1494
Internet:	www.easter-seals.org

Girl Scouts of the USA

address:	420 5th Avenue
	New York, NY 10018-2798
phone:	800-247-8319 / 1-212-852-6510
fax:	212-852-8183
Internet:	www.girlscouts.org

National Camp Association, Inc.

address: 610 Fifth Ave.
PO Box 5371
New York, NY 10185
phone: 800-966-CAMP (2267)/212-645-0653
fax: 914-354-5501
Internet: www.summercamp.org

United Way of America

address: 701 N. Fairfax Street
Alexandria, VA 22314-2045
phone: 703-836-7100
fax: 703-683-7840
Internet: www.unitedway.org

YMCA of the USA

address: 101 North Wacker Drive
Chicago, IL 60606
phone: 312-977-0031
fax: 312-977-9063
Internet: www.ymca.net

YWCA of the USA

address: Empire State Building
Suite 301
New York, NY 10118
phone: 212-273-7800
fax: 212-465-2281
Internet: www.ywca.org

2. Internet web sites for finding camps

Web pages are revised frequently, and new sites are added to the Internet daily. Some of these sites may have changed, for better or for worse, from the time we researched them. Nevertheless, this list will get you started on a web search for the best overnight camp.

We also recommend using the commercial search engine of your choice and typing in the keywords "camp," "summer camp," "resident camp," or "overnight camp" to see what you find. If you're searching for a specialty or special needs camp, type in the corresponding keywords, such as "soccer camp," "music camp," or "diabetes camp." Some common search engines include www.yahoo.com, www.excite.com, www.hotbot.com, www.infoseek.com, and www.altavista.com.

Some Internet sites and search engines include only the camps that pay for advertising; others include only camps of a particular type. To be thorough, your Internet search should include visits to multiple web pages.

- **American Camping Association (www.ACAcamps.org):** This huge site offers lots of information compiled by camping professionals. You'll find the information for parents, including the Interactive Camp Database (the on-line version of the ACA's *Guide to Accredited Camps*), particularly helpful. You'll also find job listings, camp rentals, media resources, a link to the ACA bookstore, and a special "Kids Only" section with links to other camp-related web sites for kids. Only ACA-accredited camps are listed.

- **Association of Jewish Sponsored Camps (www.jewishcamps.org):** This small site has sections about the AJSC, youth camps, adult camps, camps for children with special needs, and a staff information section. You can also send e-mail to the association for more information and get AJSC news updates. Only AJSC camps are listed, of which fewer than 40 are for kids.

- **Boy Scouts of America (www.bsa.scouting.org):** This site has general information on Tiger Cubs, Cub Scouts, Boy Scouts, Varsity Scouting, Venturing, and Eagle Scouts. You can search for BSA camps, but this site is best equipped to help you find your local BSA council. These local councils are the best places to look for information on BSA camps. You can also find information about other BSA activities, official gear, and magazines.

- **Camp & Conference (www.camping.org):** This site provides a search engine to help you find camps by name, location, type, and ACA accreditation. It features a "Camp-o'-the-Week" and links to on-line magazines, camping associations and organizations, and information on environmental and outdoor education. The site is limited to those camps that pay the yearly advertising fee.

- **Camp Channel (www.campchannel.com):** The Camp Channel offers a large, well organized search engine for camps in the US, Canada, and around the world. You can search for camps by name, location, type, and featured activities. You'll also find information for campers and directors, a job board, links to on-line camp equipment vendors (shopforcamp.com), and a featured "Camp of the Month." The site is limited to those camps that pay the yearly advertising fee.

- **Campfinders (www.campfinders.com):** Campfinders is a free referral service. According to the site, they visit each camp in their database. Nearly all the camps are in the eastern United States. It appears that you contact them and they get back in touch with you to find a camp that suits your preferences.

- **Camp Fire Boys and Girls (www.campfire.org):** Camp Fire Boys and Girls is a United Way Agency that sponsors many different youth camping programs. Currently, this site doesn't have a large, easily searchable database of camps. However, you can find the address and phone number of your local chapter on this site, and then send away for camp information.

- **CampNet (www.campnet.org):** This site provides a database of over 8000 day and overnight camps. Like the Peterson's guide, the information on CampNet was compiled by gathering questionnaires from thousands of camps. You can search for camps by name, location, type, and featured activities. Although it's supposedly accessing a large database, the CampNet search engine seemed to have trouble finding some camps that meet even the most basic criteria.

- **Camp Page (www.camppage.com):** This site features traditional camps with general programs, and thus will be of less use to parents searching for specialty camps. Camps are categorized by gender and geographic location (United States and Canada). The selection seems to be average in size. The page also contains links to other camping sites.

- **CampSearch (www.campsearch.com):** CampSearch claims to have over 2000 camps in its database. At the time of our research, the database contained about 850 camps in the United States, 500 in Canada, and many in other countries. The search engine allows parents to search by gender or age, cost, time of year, length of stay, type of camp, or location. You'll also find numerous camping links.

- **Christian Connections (camping.tcmnet.com):** As the name implies, this site lists Christian camps and retreat centers. Users can search by state, province, or country. At the time of our research, the selection of camps was somewhat limited.

- **Family.com Super Camp Guide (www.family.go.com/Features/family_0000_01/locl/Camps):** This site has a lot of summer camp information for parents as well as links to general parenting information. Camp listings are by region or metropolitan area and do not seem to cover the whole United States, so this site may be better for some users than for others. Some of the regional listings are quite extensive, but search capabilities are limited.

- **4-H (www.4-h.org/fourweb/):** 4-H camps are sponsored at the state and local level. This site will help you find your local 4-H chapter, which can then provide information on camps.

- **Frost's Summer Camp Guide Online (www.frosts.com):** This site offers information on finding camps, articles for parents and kids, answers to commonly asked questions, and career-oriented camp programs. You can search for camps by name, location, and type. Information here may be more up-to-date than the printed Frost's *Summer Camp Guide*. Both accredited and non-accredited camps pay to be listed in Frost's database of about 1000 day and overnight camps. The search engine is efficient and provides lots of details on individual camps in the U.S. and Canada.

- **Girl Scouts USA (www.girlscouts.com):** Like 4-H, Girl Scouts sponsors camps at the state and local level. This site will help you find your local Girl Scout chapter, which can then provide information on camps.

- **InterCamp (www.intercamp.com):** This site, sponsored by an Internet consulting firm, describes itself as "an online meeting place for those involved in the camping industry or interested in it." It offers an on-line directory of about 2000 day and overnight camps, searchable by name, location, price, type, and featured activities. There are also chat rooms, where former campers can reminisce and parents can ask questions of camp directors.

- **KidsCamps (www.kidscamps.com):** This large site offers a well organized search engine that allows you to look for camps by name, location, type, and featured activities. You can also search for family camps, resort camps, and "tours and adventures," as well as job listings, information on camp conference centers, and adult camps. Finally, the site offers a camp store (CampersMall.com) and links to various camp associations.

- **National Camp Association (www.summercamp.org):** The NCA describes itself as "a public guidance and referral service which recommends the finest summer camps throughout the country and abroad." Whereas the ACA is run by camp directors, the NCA is an independent organization supported by affiliated camps. Instead of a database of camps, the NCA site has an "On-Line Camp Selection Guide." This electronic form allows you to send your name, address, phone number, and other contact information to the NCA. Soon thereafter, an NCA advisor will contact you to discuss overnight camp.

- **Peterson's Summer Opportunities (www.petersons.com/ summerop):** Like the book of the same name, this enormous site lists not only summer camps, but also a variety of other academic and travel opportunities for children and adolescents. You can search for camps and other activities by name, region, activity, and type. The site also contains job listings, information for international students, a link to the ACA camp search engine, and an on-line bookstore.

- **Vincent-Curtis Education Register (www.vincentcurtis.com):** This is an on-line version of *The Educational Register*, published by Vincent-Curtis and detailing about 1000 private schools and summer camps in the United States, Canada, and Europe. You can search for summer school programs only, camps only, or both. Users can search for camps by age, gender, and location.

3. ACA section offices

The American Camping Association has 24 regional section offices that can provide information on overnight camps in your area. Many offices also have a Speaker's Bureau and a network of "Ambassadors" available to give presentations to community groups, schools, church groups, and the like. Contact information occasionally changes, but you can get up-to-the-minute section information on the Internet at: www.ACAcamps.org/section.htm

Chesapeake: *(Maryland & Washington, D.C.)*

address:	Patuxent River 4-H Center
	18405 Queen Anne Road
	Upper Marlboro, MD 20774
phone:	800-653-1409/301-218-6468
e-mail:	canterfamily@erols.com
Internet:	www.ACAcamps.org/ck

Coronado: *(Nevada, Utah, Arizona, & New Mexico)*

address:	1814 West Libby Street
	Phoenix, AZ 85023-2383
phone:	800-871-0270 (for messages)
	602-557-1142/602-942-1616
fax:	602-968-1159
e-mail:	glpauley@apollogrp.edu
Internet:	www.ACAcamps.org/co

Evergreen: *(Montana, Northern Idaho, Washington & Alaska)*

address:	6523 California Avenue SW #305
	Seattle, WA 98136-1833
phone:	206-892-3906
fax:	206-935-4424
e-mail:	tnielsen7@aol.com
Internet:	www.ACAcamps.org/eg

Great Rivers: *(Iowa, Kansas, Missouri, Nebraska)*

address:	P.O. Box 190
	West Burlington, IA 52655
phone:	888-RIVER83 (748-3783)
Internet:	www.ACAcamps.org/gr

Keystone Regional: *(Pennsylvania & Delaware)*

address:	P.O. Box 86
	Jenkintown, PA 19046
phone:	888-917-CAMP (2267)/215-886-5385
fax:	215-885-7334
e-mail:	acakeystone@i-bob.com
Internet:	www.ACAcamps.org/kr

Heart of the South: *(Alabama, Arkansas, Kentucky, Louisiana, Mississippi, & Tennessee)*

address:	Tate's Day Camp
	1031 Cedar Bluff Road
	Knoxville, TN 37923
phone:	423-690-9208
fax:	423-693-8532
e-mail:	stevel@aol.com
Internet:	www.ACA camps.org/cb

Illinois: *(Illinois only; see also St. Louis section)*

address:	67 East Madison Street #1406
	Chicago, IL 60603-3010
phone:	312-332-0833 /312-332-2497
fax:	312-332-4011
e-mail:	acail@imaxx.net
Internet:	www.ACAcamps.org/il

Indiana: *(Indiana only)*

address:	2001 South Bridgeport Road
	Indianapolis, IN 46231
phone:	888-620-2267
fax:	317-241-5729
e-mail:	acaindiana@yahoo.com
Internet:	www.ACAcamps.org/in

Michigan: *(Michigan only)*

address:	174 E 32nd Street
	Holland, MI 49423
phone:	800-852-8368 (Michigan only)/616-393-8591
fax:	616-393-8616
e-mail:	heathere@michigancamps-aca.org
Internet:	www.ACAcamps.org/mi OR
	www.michigancamps-aca.org

New England: *(Maine, New Hampshire, Vermont, Massachusetts, Connecticut, & Rhode Island)*

address:	214 North Maine Street #104
	Natick, MA 01760-1131
phone:	800-446-4494 /508-647-CAMP (2267)
fax:	508-647-4890
e-mail:	camp@acane-camps.org
Internet:	www.ACAcamps.org/ne OR
	www.acane-camps.org

New Jersey: *(New Jersey only)*

address:	c/o Camp Mary Heart
	21 O'Brian Road
	Hackettstown, NJ 07840
phone:	908-852-0145 /908-852-3896
fax:	908-852-9263
e-mail:	acanj@garden.net
Internet:	www.ACAcamps.org/nj OR
	www.garden.net/user/acanj

New York: *(For the following counties: Sullivan, Ulster, Dutchess, Putnam, Orange, Westchester, Rockland, Richmond, Kings, Queens, Bronx, Manhattan, Nassau, Suffolk; see also Upstate New York section)*

address:	12 West 31st Street
	New York, NY 10001
phone:	800-777-CAMP (2267)/212-268-7822
fax:	212-594-1684
e-mail:	camp@aca-ny.org
Internet:	www.ACAcamps.org/ny OR
	www.aca-ny.org

Northern California: *(Northern California only)*

address:	2915 Kerner Blvd Suite A
	San Rafael, CA 94901
phone:	800-362-2236 /415-459-2235
fax:	415-459-6298
e-mail:	aca@vkam.com
Internet:	www.ACAcamps.org/nc

Northland: *(Minnesota, North Dakota, & South Dakota)*

address:	4132 88th Lane NE
	Circle Pines, MN 55014
phone:	800-842-0308 /612-784-5400
fax:	612-784-5400
e-mail:	kkalbright@juno.com
Internet:	www.ACAcamps.org/nl

Ohio: *(Ohio only)*

address:	6320 Greenwood Pkwy #405
	Northfield, OH 44067
phone:	800-837-2269 /440-585-7736 ext.30
fax:	440-585-7747
e-mail:	acaohio@juno.com
Internet:	www.ACAcamps.org/oh

Oregon Trail: *(Oregon & Southern Idaho)*

address:	Columbia River GSC
	P.O. Box 2427
	Lake Oswego, OR 97035-0096
phone:	800-338-5248 /503-293-6716
fax:	503-598-6556
e-mail:	bussk@juliette.org
Internet:	www.ACAcamps.org/ot

Rocky Mountain: *(Colorado & Wyoming)*

address:	P.O. Box 268
	Indian Hills, CO 80454
phone:	888-926-CAMP (2267)
fax:	970-586-6078
e-mail:	molly@genevaglen.org
Internet:	www.ACAcamps.org/rm

Southeastern: *(Georgia, North Carolina, South Carolina, & Florida)*

address:	c/o Appalachian State University
	Dept. of HLES, Varsity Gym
	Boone, NC 28608
phone:	828-262-2840
fax:	828-262-6545
e-mail:	acase@appstate.edu
Internet:	www.ACAcamps.org/se

Southern California: *(Southern California & Hawaii)*

address:	22231 Mulholland Highway # 212
	Calabasas, CA 91302-5123
phone:	818-223-9232/818-223-9316
fax:	818-223-9326
e-mail:	acasocalif@aol.com
Internet	www.ACAcamps.org/sc

St. Louis: *(Eastern Missouri & Southern Illinois; see also Illinois section)*

address:	Shagbark GSC
	P.O. Box 549
	304 N. 14th Street
	Herrin, IL 62948
phone:	888-464-7553/618-942-3164
fax:	618-942-7153
e-mail:	shagbark@midwest.net
Internet:	www.ACAcamps.org/sl

Texcoma: *(Texas & Oklahoma)*

address:	2700 Meacham Blvd
	Fort Worth, TX 76137
phone:	817-831-2111 ext. 155
fax:	817-831-5070
Internet:	www.ACAcamps.org/to OR www.acatx.org

Upstate New York: *(Upstate New York; see also New York section)*

address:	2072 Four Rod Road
	East Aurora, NY 14052
phone:	716-655-3603
e-mail:	usnyaca@aol.com
Internet:	www.ACAcamps.org/un

Virginias: *(Virginia & West Virginia)*

address:	7862 Apache Ridge Ct.
	Masassas, VA 20109
phone:	703-368-8815
fax:	703-368-8715
e-mail:	acavirginias@yahoo.com
Internet:	www.ACAcamps.org/va

Wisconsin: *(Wisconsin only)*

address:	6255 North Santa Monica Blvd.
	Milwaukee, WI 53217-4353
phone:	414-967-8185 /445-5695
fax:	414-964-0922
e-mail:	acawicmp@win.bright.net
Internet:	www.ACAcamps.org/wi

4. Canadian camp contacts

The CCA and its provincial branches can be accessed on the Internet via KidsCamps.com. Go to KidsCamps.com/canadian-campiing/index.html

Canadian Camping Association/Association Des Camps Du Canada

address:	1810 Avenue Road, Suite 303
	Toronto, Ontario, Canada M5M 3Z2
phone:	416-781-4717
fax:	416-781-7875
e-mail:	canada@kidscamps.com

Alberta Camping Association

address:	Percy Page Centre,
	11759 Groat Road,
	Edmonton, AB T5M 3K6
phone:	403-453-8570
fax:	403-453-8553
e-mail:	abcamp@freenet.edmonton.ab.ca

British Columbia Camping Association

address:	c/o Sasamat Outdoor Centre
	3302 Senkler Road
	Belcarra, BC V3H 4S3
phone:	604-931-6449/(604)-939-8522
fax:	604-875-6760

Camping Association of Nova Scotia

address:	Box 3243 South, Halifax
	NS, B3J 3H5
phone:	902-865-3523
fax:	902-864-7543.

Manitoba Camping Association

address:	194a Sherbrook Street
	Winnipeg, MB R3C 2B6
phone:	204-784-1134
fax:	204-784-1133

New Brunswick Camping Committee: Park Office Centre

address:	440 Wilsey Road, Ste 105
	Fredricton, NB E3B 7G5
phone:	506-459-1929
fax:	506-450-6066

Newfoundland/Labrador Camping Association

address:	PO Box 50846, SS #3
	St. Johns, NF A1B 4M2
phone:	709-576-7198
fax:	709-576-8146

Ontario Camping Association

address:	1810 Avenue Road, Suite #302
	Toronto, Ontario M5M 3Z2
phone:	416-781-0525
fax:	416-781-7875

(Quebec) Association des Camps du Québec

address:	4545 ave. Pierre de Coubertain
	Case Postale 1000
	Succursale M,
	Montréal, PQ H1V 3R2
phone:	514-252-3113
fax:	514-252-1650

Saskatchewan Camping Association

address:	Box 8862
	Saskatoon, SK S7K 6S6
phone:	306-949-4141
fax:	306-949-3069

5. Resources for finding special needs camps

These contacts were obtained from the National Information Center for Children and Youth with Disabilities (NICHCY). These references, combined with an Internet search or a good resource book (see the last section of this chapter), should help you locate an excellent camp for your child with special needs.

American Burn Association

address: Information on Burn Camps
             625 N. Michigan Avenue, Ste 1530
             Chicago, IL 60611
phone: 800-548-2876
Internet: www.ameriburn.org

Annual Special Camp Guide

address: Resources for Children with Special Needs
             200 Park Avenue, South, Suite 816
             New York, NY 10003
phone: 212-677-4650 (available in English & Spanish)

Camps for Children with Attention Deficit Disorder

address: Children and Adults with Attention Deficit Disorder (CHADD)
             499 NW 70th Avenue, Suite 101
             Plantation, FL 33317
phone: 954-587-3700

Camps for Children with Diabetes

Internet: www.castleweb.com/diabetes/d_07_100.htm

Camps for Children with Spina Bifida

address: Spina Bifida Association of America
             4590 MacArthur Boulevard, NW, Suite 250
             Washington, D.C. 20007
phone: 202-944-3285/800-621-3141

The Candlelighters Childhood
Cancer Foundation (Camp List for Children with Cancer)

address: 7910 Woodmont Avenue, Suite 460
             Bethesda, MD 20814
phone: 301-657-8401

COPE's Special Education Directory

address: Creating Opportunities for Parent Empowerment (COPE)
300 I Street, NE, Suite 112
Washington, D.C. 20002

phone: 202-543-6482

Directory of Summer Camps for Children with Learning Disabilities

address: Learning Disabilities Association (LDA)
4156 Library Road
Pittsburgh, PA 15234

phone: 412-341-1515

Internet: www.ldanatl.org/store/LD_Directories.html

Easter Seals Resident Camps

address: 230 West Monroe Street
Suite 1800
Chicago, IL 60606

phone: 800-221-6827/1-312-726-6200

TDD: 312-726-4258

fax: 312-726-1494

Internet: www.easter-seals.org

National Information Center for Children and Youth with Disabilities (NICHCY)

address: P.O. Box 1492
Washington, DC 20013

phone: 800-695-0285 (Voice/TT)
202-884-8200 (Voice/TT)

e-mail: nichcy@aed.org

Internet: www.nichcy.org

Summer Camps for Children Who Are Deaf or Hard of Hearing

address: National Information Center on Deafness
Gallaudet University
800 Florida Avenue, NE
Washington, D.C. 20002

phone: 202-651-5051

Internet: www.gallaudet.edu/~nicd/142.html

6. Commercial care package vendors

Camp Pacs

address:	224 Main Street
	Brevard, NC 28712
phone:	800-248-CAMP
fax:	828-885-2925
e-mail:	mainstltd@citcom.net

Sealed With a Kiss

address:	P.O. Box 2063
	6709 Tildenwood Lane
	Rockville, MD 20847
phone:	800-888-7925 (SWAK)/301-468-2604
fax:	301-468-2605
Internet:	www.swakpack.com

The Wrinkled Egg

address:	P.O. Box 373
	2710 US Hwy 25
	Flat Rock, NC 28731
phone:	800-736-3998/828-696-3998
fax:	828-697-6760
e-mail:	chickenchat@wrinkledegg.com
Internet:	www.wrinkledegg.com

7. Name labels, laundry bags, and other camp supplies

You can find camp supplies at most discount department stores, Army surplus stores, and drug stores. The vendors below are some of the best, but this not a complete list. You can also find vendors on the Internet. For example, both L. L. Bean and REI have huge web-based catalogues.

Name Stamps and Labels
Best Name Tape Co.

address:	P.O. Box 1228
	Nashua, N.H. 03061
phone:	603-882-3957
fax:	603-889-8705
e-mail:	bestname@aol.com
Internet:	www.kidscamps.com/marketplace/bestnametape/

Caring Products/The Caring Center

address:	5519 Clairemont Mesa Blvd.
	Suite 333
	San Diego
phone:	800-STAMP KIT (782-6754)
fax:	619-576-2304
Internet:	www.campstamp.com

The Label Company

address:	PO Box 249
	Bowdon GA 30108
phone:	770- 258-7275
e-mail:	msteed@steedco.com
Internet:	www.steedco.com/tlc.html

The Name-On Company

address:	3401 North "I" Street
	Philadelphia, PA 19134
phone:	215-426-2121

Sterling Name Tape Company

address:	9 Willow Street
	P.O. Box 939
	Winsted, Ct 06098
phone:	860-379-5142
fax:	860-379-0394/800-654-5210
e-mail:	colwash@esslink.com
Internet:	www.kidscamps.com/marketplace/sterling-name/

Trunks and Other Camp Supplies
Bunk Line

address:	431 Commerce Lane
	West Berlin, NJ 08091
phone:	800-435-6888/609-768-1129 (local)
fax:	800-435-7509/609-768-7511
e-mail:	info@bunkline.com
Internet:	www.bunkline.com

The Camper's Collection

address:	P.O. Box 272
	Pittsford, NY 14534
phone:	800-724-2531/716-381-5420
fax:	716-381-8528
Internet:	www.camperscollection.com

The Name-On Company

address:	3401 North "I" Street
	Philadelphia, PA 19134
phone:	215-426-2121

Texas Case Manufacturing

address:	P.O. Box 244
	Morgan Mill, TX 76465
phone:	800-599-5834
fax:	254-968-4725
Internet:	www.kidscamps.com/suppliers/texas-case/

Sockmonster Saks

address:	100 Springdale Road
	A3 Suite 213
	Cherry Hill, NJ 08003
phone:	609-795-9799
fax:	609-428-4004

Clothing and Outdoor Gear

The following vendors offer an enormous selection of top camping equipment. Sierra Trading Post and Campmor are primarily mail order and on-line catalogue stores, offering deep discounts on a rotating stock of clothing and outdoor gear. L. L. Bean, REI, and EMS have store locations and outlets throughout the country. Call or go on-line to order equipment or find the retail store nearest you. If your budget is tight, and you're not shopping for specialized gear, consider buying some items at a discount department store. Wherever you shop, remember that quality is important because camp is tough on clothing and other outdoor gear.

Campmor

address:	810 Route 17 North
	Paramus, NJ 07653
phone:	888-CAMPMOR (226-7667)
fax:	800-230-2153
Internet:	www.campmor.com

EMS (Eastern Mountain Sports)

address:	327 Jaffrey Rd.
	Peterborough, NH 03458
phone:	888-INFO-EMS (463-6367)
fax:	603-924-7253
Internet:	www.emsonline.com

L. L. Bean

address:	Freeport, ME 04034
phone:	800-441-5713
fax:	207-552-3080
e-mail:	LLBean@llbean.com
Internet:	www.llbean.com

REI, Inc. (Recreational Equipment, Incorporated)

address:	Sumner, WA 98352
phone:	800-426-4840
fax:	253-891-2523
Internet:	www.rei.com

Sierra Trading Post

address:	5025 Campstool Rd.
	Cheyenne, WY 82007-1898
phone:	800-713-4534
fax:	800-378-8946
Internet:	www.SierraTradingPost.com

8. Resource books

These books are excellent sources of information on summer camps, summer programs, camp-related issues, and camp history. Most are available through bookstores, the Internet, or by calling the publisher. Also check your local college, university, or public library.

Books That List Different Camps

Guide to ACA-Accredited Camps

publisher:	American Camping Association
	5000 Sate Road 65 North
	Martinsville, IN 46151-7902
phone:	800-428-CAMP
Internet:	www.ACAcamps.org

Frost's Summer Camp Guide

publisher:	Frost's
	50 Parkhill Road
	Harrington Park, NJ 07640
phone:	201-784-7662
Internet:	www.frosts.com

Peterson's Summer Opportunities for Kids & Teenagers

publisher:	Peterson's
	Princeton, NJ
phone:	800-338-3282 (outside the U.S. and Canada:
	609-243-9111)
Internet:	www.petersons.com/summerop/ssector.html

Books for Children and Families About Safe Touch

A Better Safe Than Sorry Book: A Family Guide for Sexual Assault Prevention by Sol & Judith Gordon

This book is good for children between ages 4 and 10. At the end of the book, there is an excellent section written just for parents.

The Right Touch: A Read-Aloud Story to Help Prevent Child Sexual Abuse by Sandy Kleven

The storybook format makes it easy for parents to communicate the important messages, and is best for young children between ages 4 and 8.

The Safe Child Book: A Commonsense Approach to Protecting Children and Teaching Children to Protect Themselves
by Sherryll K. Kraizer

One of the best overall safety books for children and parents, with a good section on preventing unwanted touch.

The Safe Zone: A Kid's Guide to Personal Safety by Donna Chaiet & Francine Russell

> An outstanding overall safety book, especially for older children ages 8 to 14. Easy for kids to read by themselves or with their parents.

Books and Sources on the History of Camping

Building Character in the American Boy: The Boy Scouts, YMCA, and Their Forerunners, 1870-1920 by David I. Macleod

Eleanor Eells' History of Organized Camping, The First 100 Years by Eleanor Eells

100 Years of YMCA Camping by Eugene A. Turner, Jr.

American Museum of Natural History

> Central Park West at 79th
> New York, NY 10024-5192
> www.amn..org

Ernest Thompson Seton Institute, Inc.

> 111 Pacifica, Suite 250
> Irvine, CA 92618
> www.etsetoninstitute.org

Index

More from Perspective Publishing

Perspective Publishing is a small independent publishing company which helps parents with the problems you face every day: discipline, friendship problems, talking with your kids, balancing work and family, challenging and inspiring your kids.

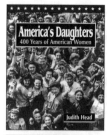

AMERICA'S DAUGHTERS: 400 Years of American Women
by Judith Head

This easy-to-read yet carefully researched history of American women from the 1600s to today is illustrated with 150 photos and period drawings, and gives children and adults both an overview of what life was like for women, and profiles of more than 50 individual women, both famous and not so well known.

ISBN: 0-9622036-8-8 Paperback. 8"x10"; 136 pages; $16.95

Win the Whining War & Other Skirmishes: A family peace plan
by Cynthia Whitham, MSW

This easy-to-use guide helps parents increase cooperation and reduce conflict with children ages 2-12. Step-by-step, parents learn how to cut out all the annoying behavior (tantrums, teasing, dawdling, interrupting, complaining, etc.) that drives them crazy.

ISBN: 0-9622036-3-7, paperback. 6"x9"; 208 pages; $13.95

"The Answer is NO": Saying it and sticking to it
by Cynthia Whitham, MSW

Tackling twenty-six situations that plague parents of 2 to 12-year-olds, this book helps parents define their values, build good parenting habits, and set firm, fair limits. Bedtime, pets, makeup, music, TV, homework, and designer clothes are just a few of the problems covered.

ISBN: 0-9622036-4-5, paperback. 6"x9"; 224 pages; $13.95l

Survival Tips for Working Moms: 297 REAL Tips from REAL Moms
by Linda Goodman Pillsbury

Full of examples of how the tips actually work in real families, this is a light but no-nonsense practical resource thast can help every working mom. From chores to childcare, errands to exercise, this book makes life easier. Almost 100 cartoons make this a book you can't put down.

ISBN: 0-9622036-5-3, paperback. 6"x9"; 192 pages; $10.95

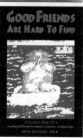

Good Friends Are Hard to Find: Help your child find, make and keep friends
by Fred Frankel, Ph.D.

Step-by-step, parents learn to help their 5 to 12-year-olds make friends and solve problems with other kids. This guide also offers concrete help for teasing, bullying and meanness, both for the child who is picked on and for the tormentor. Based on UCLA's world renowned Children's Social Skills Program, this book teaches clinically tested techniques that really work.

ISBN: 0-9622036-7-X, paperback. 6"x9"; 242 pages; $13.95

Order now: 1-800-330-5851 or www.familyhelp.com